12 UNDENIABLE LAWS FOR BEING A KINGDOM OF HEAVEN AMBASSADOR

WHAT THE BIBLE SAYS THAT CAN SECURE SUCCESS IN YOUR DEPLOYMENT TO THE EARTH

BY: TIFFANY DOMENA

Copyright © 2015 by Tiffany Domena.

www.kingdomofheavenambassador.com

TABLE OF CONTENTS

Preface v

Introduction 1

Chapter One: Take Your Deployment Seriously 5

Chapter Two: Take Possession of What's Yours 19

Chapter Three: Divorce The Devil 39

Chapter Four: Know Your Benefits 75

Chapter Five: Be Strong In Spiritual Self-Defense 91

Chapter Six: Plunder The Enemy! 107

Chapter Seven: Be Strong In Offensive Spiritual
    Warfare Tactics 117

Chapter Eight: Walk With YHWH, Not Behind Him! 129

Chapter Nine: Store Treasure In Heaven 153

Chapter Ten: Surrender The Eyes Of Your Mind 165

Chapter Eleven: See The Aerial View 185

Chapter Twelve: Make treaties 205

Divine Commission For Being A Kingdom Of
Heaven Ambassador 217

About The Author 221

One Last Thing… 223

PREFACE

Are you a "Christian" or are you a disciple of Yeshua? Pagan activity has seeped into many facets of the teachings of the Messiah. In the Laodicean council the customs that he taught were uniformly manipulated (look it up). On many occasions in history, the name of The Most High and His Son have been manipulated under the excuse of "translation" or "transliteration", and even at times to gain intentional praise to gods with similarly called or pronounced names such as "Lord", "Christ", "Jesus", or "God". In this book, I will be setting Him apart by referencing Him by the Hebrew names that no other god can claim.

If you read any of my previously published books, when reading this book, you will find a large metamorphosis of concepts have been added to me as I made myself a living sacrifice and willing vessel to remove things that were unlike YHWH. Many of the concepts will be expanded, some will be properly put in context, and culturally common sins correlating with undermining the importance of Torah will be pruned. In this book (unlike my others) the Hebrew name of The Most High God, YHWH will be used, and His Son will be called "Yeshua" as these are the historically sound, unmanipulated names.

If you are unwilling to reshape your paradigm, be a living sacrifice (meaning "a life not your own but of Yeshua"), and demonstrate allegiance in action, this book may be offensive and unfitting for you.

The things written about in this book were not practices that I was raised implementing. Rather, I was raised in a Christian non-denominational church that engaged in many practices and teachings that are common to the Evangelical worldview of this time. In my search for truth, I have prayed to YHWH that He would reveal truth to me, and the results of that are written about in this book.

Are you a "Christian" or are you in a relationship with Yeshua? Do you talk about the Kingdom of YHWH or is the Kingdom of YHWH accessible and demonstrated in your life? As in the days of Noah, today we live in a murky and dark world; one where people associate themselves with Yeshua, but truly don't know Him. We are truly in the end times, and most people are blinded by the entertainment of Satan. The majority of those who wear Jesus' name do not satisfy the Savior whom they reference with their lives. He said to choose whether you are going to be hot or cold because even the lukewarm will be thrown to hell. Don't be one of them!

In 2 Corinthians 5:20 it says, "We are therefore Christ's ambassadors, as though YHWH were making his appeal through us. We implore you on Christ's behalf: Be reconciled to YHWH." Do you know what it means to be a government ambassador? You have been deployed to this Earth to offer resources to the Earth's inhabitants. Are you prepared? Do you know the Kingdom's resources? Do you know how to use them? Do you have a relationship with your King?

Not a single person has been sent to this Earth without reason. Many of those who come become deceived by alternative views because your enemy (unlike many of the world's battles) seeks to only deter you from YHWH's will with the gradual goal of killing you; rather than the world's enemies who may present themselves in a much more noticeable form. For most people, they are easily overtaken by the enemy because they are taught to see from the physical eye, and with the enemy being a spirit being, he deceives them using spiritual senses. It is the spiritual enemies who cause the most damage; they get all of the intelligence about you, and this is true of the spiritual battle you are in.

This book will help you to walk in strength and dignity towards success in your deployment here on the Earth. The time is over for you to walk partially yielded (lukewarm) or not at all (cold). Your eternity is at risk simply because you walk in ignorance! If you choose to continue reading, you will find insight about your Kingdom's resources, how to use them, and how to make them accessible to others so the Kingdom of Heaven benefits can be afforded to more of Earth's inhabitants. The world needs liberation. Are you ready to bring it to them? If so, continue reading. I look forward to walking alongside you on this journey as we raise the temperature in your spiritual life and raise the standard of the Kingdom Ambassadors on this Earth.

Within this text are:

- 12 Laws For Success in your deployment as a Kingdom of Heaven Ambassador

- My personal insight as a diplomat who has discovered things about the Kingdom

- Action Steps To Push You Closer To Your Potential As A Kingdom Appointed Ambassador

- Stories To Subconsciously Reprogram Your Mind

- And, Prayers That Will Manifest Heaven On Earth

INTRODUCTION

Growing up in a defiant economy where science, the entertainment industry, the banking system, and the government create the majority of standards of right and wrong, many of the people of our world have been spoon fed lies by the enemy. Even worse, Christianity has become so demoralized and absent of power the occult has grown in massive ways, and currently dominates the institutionalized world. Yeshua said Satan was thrown down from Heaven and currently is the Prince of the air, but with his ways being a norm, how does one fervently choose to abandon his plot for their lives? How can a foreigner stand in a world that is so absent from those seeking the spirit of truth? With these questions in mind, I began studying for this book.

On several occasions, I have accidentally run into the works of Satan. I was raised with YHWH-fearing parents who did their best to abstain from Satanic influence, but because he is so diverse in his approach, he still seeped thru. I began praying and asking YHWH for revelation. I aligned with His promises of protection, His promises of power, and I realized He has given His signet ring to His ambassadors who walk uprightly. Most Christian people are unaware of who Yeshua truly is and the level of authority that has been granted to them, but I have good news, "The Kingdom of YHWH is at hand!"

Liberty is the evidence Heaven is present (2 Corinthians 3:17). Within the realm of the Holy Spirit is liberty. "The Kingdom of YHWH is at hand", means the world of YHWH is within reach. He is accessible! My secret to you...you were created to be a gate of the Kingdom of YHWH! Yeshua tore the veil between Heaven and Earth during his baptism when the Father sent the Holy Spirit down upon him. This became a norm for all Christian people where the Holy Spirit has access, and they have access to an open Heaven above them where they can freely visit the place that is absent from evil and bring things from Heaven to Earth, and ascend beyond the Earthly circumstances thru relationship with YHWH. When He died and rose again, He tore the physical veil between the outer court and the Holy of Holies making the throne of YHWH available to us all.

In Matthew 28:18-20, you were given a mandate, orders from the Kingdom of Heaven to colonize the Earth as an ambassador of Yeshua. It says:

And Yeshua came and said to them, "All authority in heaven and on earth has been given to me. Go therefore and make disciples of all nations, baptizing them in the name of the Father and of the Son and of the Holy Spirit, and teaching them to obey everything I have commanded you. And remember, I am with you always, to the end of the age."

As Ambassadors of the Messiah, commissioned by Yeshua to go to all of the nations, baptizing in the name of the Father, and preaching the things he taught-- you have been given His signet ring to administer the Kingdom of Heaven and bring liberation to others. Every time YHWH speaks, He releases the reality of His world in you. It's the glory of YHWH to hide things, but it is the glory of Kings to search them out. We have the ability to inherit increase in our identities when we search out the matters of the Kingdom.

Mark Parsons said, "Your life is an embassy of the Kingdom of Heaven". This book is intended to bring clarity on how to operate as an ambassador and embassy of Heaven. Servants are concerned more about doing what was said, but as a Kingdom of Heaven Ambassador, you are also a friend of God the Father, His son, Yeshua, and the Holy Spirit, therefore, you are concerned about what moves the heart of YHWH.

Be blessed!

Tiffany Domena

CHAPTER ONE

TAKE YOUR DEPLOYMENT SERIOUSLY

"YHWH wants us so connected with his presence on the inside of us, which is connected to heaven, that it is releasing the sound of heaven through us. 'On earth as it is in heaven': the sound of heaven, the light of heaven, the power of heaven would be released through us."
-Mike Parsons

The Author's Assignment To Babylon

In April 2010, I was deployed to Iraq. The Pentagon participates in the ongoing process of gaining intelligence--or whereabouts and status reports on other countries--then they create a strategy that includes how many military personnel will be needed to support each military mission, and what equipment will be necessary to send them with. Accordingly, I found out my skill set was needed in Iraq one month prior to when I needed to leave. I was given a checklist of many things I needed to do before I left. I had training to accomplish to get familiar with the Middle Eastern culture. I had ammunition training, survival training, and many other trainings to attend prior to departure. I had to get training on my job, so during my deployment, I could work at maximum capacity for my specialty. I had to get vaccinations and go to many medical appointments to ensure my health could withstand the deployment. When the time came for me to take off, I left with a lot of knowledge and preparation, several uniforms, more than one pair of boots, toiletries, ammunition, guns, and books to supplement my knowledge. I left with about 12 other military personnel, and we traveled from San Antonio, Texas to Iraq together.

The Sacrifice In Service

Similar to my experience as a military troop, you are deployed here to the Earth from the Kingdom of Heaven. YHWH has sent you to the Earth prepared for the assignment to which you have been assigned. He has given you talents, passions, wisdom, demographics, psychographics, spiritual armor, and everything else necessary to fulfill your assignment.

With my enlistment into the military, I had to sign a contract stating my willingness to defend the country even if it required me to lay down my life. All government employees have to sign a comparable contract stating that they will not divulge information given to them by the government, they must not ally with enemies of the country they are defending, they should make necessary sacrifices to align themselves with the ideology of the country, or be severely punished for opposition.

Every person has been placed on the Earth to administer the Kingdom of Heaven. By way of Satan's intentional tactics, some people will become distracted by ulterior paths: complacency, idolatry, sorcery (sometimes intentional or sometimes by way of drug use), immorality, and others. At the end of this life, we are all faced with the day when we stand accountable for how well we were as stewards of the gift of life, talents, connections, and resources. Those who will be rewarded are those who have multiplied what they were given; those who have exercised the assignment as a Kingdom ambassador well. Yeshua said:

"To those who use well what they are given, even more will be given, and they will have an abundance. But from those who do nothing, even what little they have will be taken away. Now throw this useless servant into outer darkness, where there will be weeping and gnashing of teeth.'"

Similar to the contract I signed with the military, YHWH set laws before you, and you must decide who you will follow. For the military, I had to wear a uniform daily, I was taught conduct, I had attendance requirements, training I had to do, and many other standards to uphold on-duty and off-duty.

As an ambassador of the Kingdom of Heaven, you are required to abide by similar statutes. You are to present yourself as a living sacrifice to the King. Your life, your works, and your ways should no longer be directed by your own thoughts and will, but rather, you sacrifice in allegiance to your citizenry in Heaven.

In the Old Testament, the priest had to prepare an unblemished lamb to atone for the sins of Israel. Similarly, Romans 12:1 says:

"And so, dear brothers and sisters, I plead with you to give your bodies to YHWH because of all he has done for you. Let them be a living and holy sacrifice—the kind he will find acceptable. This is truly the way to worship him."

This means that as ambassadors of Heaven, we must live a distinguished lifestyle as an act of worship to our King. Just as the lamb was sacrificed procedurally, we must also yield ourselves to the responsibilities of the assignment. For the sacrificed lamb, the priest was required to:

- Slit the throat - We must abandon vain speaking. Any way that we emanate thoughts of our own will, we must subject to the authority of YHWH.

- Heads chopped off - We dethrone anything that currently leads our lives and take Yeshua as the head; the leader and authoritarian. We no longer make decisions without subjecting them to the authority of Heaven.

- Remove the skin - Any protective coverings that are placed over us must be removed. Mike Parsons said, "We cannot have defense mechanisms, protection mechanisms and our own self-righteousness as a barrier: we have to be vulnerable and transparent before YHWH, and before others."

- Slit open the body - We must become open and willing to display our inner workings; our most vulnerable assets.

- Clean the inner parts - Our hearts, minds, cells and organs that disseminate influence thru our bodies must be submitted for cleansing. Thoughts, intentions, our framework, and nutrients must be examined and adjusted to ensure we grow the ability to tap into the frequency of YHWH; the frequency of righteousness.

- Chop off the legs- Our mobility must be subject to Yeshua. We no longer walk on our own paths or ways, but we are carried by the orders of righteousness thru Yeshua.

He has deployed you to the Earth to offer the inhabitants the best in His storehouse, to end war, to end poverty, sickness, and disease by submission to Yeshua the Messiah. Are you a prepared diplomat to transmit His message to the Earth's inhabitants? Are your views on foreign policy in line with the King? Have you exercised your rights as a Kingdom of Heaven citizen?

Administration of the Eternal Kingdom

In her book, *No Higher Honor,* Condoleezza Rice talks about how she developed a relationship with George W. Bush before the days of his presidency. She flew on more than one occasion in response to his invitation, and was hosted to stayed at his home, partook in some leisure outings (to include fishing, exercising, and specialty meals). They would discuss foreign policy, political influence of previous government diplomats, and their ideas about what should or could be done to help the American government. Over the course of their relationship, they discovered they had many common beliefs on government. Also, they discovered they would be able to compensate for one another's weaknesses and accent one another's strengths. In response to their established relationship, when President Bush ran for the presidency, he requested Dr. Rice to accompany him on his campaign, and later, she became the Secretary of State for the Bush Administration.

The Secretary of State position is very comparable to an ambassador in a monarchy. Maybe you were unaware of the introduction you had with the King, but let me candidly tell you, He is very aware of you. He has chosen you as a part of Heaven's administration. He packed you up, appointed a womb, and sent you fully qualified to fill a unique role for the Kingdom of Heaven. You have been appointed by the King who has been on the throne from the beginning, and will remain on the throne eternally. Some ambassadors have done an outstanding job in their deployment on the Earth while some will receive their judgment beyond the grave. Which will you be?

Kingdom of Heaven Foreign Policy

Your King is absolute and you can learn of His views on foreign policy thru face to face communion and in His word. His message to immigrants of the Earth is written from the beginning to the end of the Bible, and it continues as you open your heart to hear Him speak to you now. He made a covenant with you and all who become Kingdom citizens. Genesis 1:26-28 says you are created in the image and likeness of the Almighty God. You have been given complete rule and dominion over the fish of the sea, the birds of the air, the beasts of the field, and every creeping thing on the Earth. You are a representation of the authority of YHWH on this Earth, and as such, you were designed to rule this planet.

YHWH is not happy with diseases that prevail on this Earth, He is not happy with conflicts amongst the Earth's inhabitants, He is not happy with lack, and He is especially unhappy with man's views of their King. He sent His son to overcome every evil.

As a child of YHWH, you are joint heir to the Kingdom. You have been deployed to this Earth to supply to the inhabitants a gate to eternity; a dose of Heaven on Earth. Your responsibility is to free those who are captive to torment, debt, bondage, depression, poverty, sickness, and other chains that the kingdom in darkness places on their citizens.

In response to the epidemics of the Earth, your King has said, He has set before the inhabitants the way of life and the way of death. (Jeremiah 21:8) He made laws as demonstrations of the inward workings of the heart. When you introduce the commands of YHWH to others, they are privy to abide or forsake; thus choosing life or death (eternally).

Kingdom of Heaven laws

Every Kingdom has laws. Most kingdoms administer laws to restrict your ability, but rather the Kingdom of Heaven has administered laws to expand your ability. They are your marriage covenant with the son of YHWH. The laws of YHWH give you details about how you can maintain spirit to spirit intimacy with Yeshua. When you abide by the laws, you can maintain an intimate place with the Father and His son where you can gain insight about the desires of His heart for you and His creation. When you adhere to them, you are able to access the full benefit of the Kingdom, but when you do not, you have limited access to the Kingdom's benefits. The Kingdom of Heaven is by far more abundant in citizenship benefits than any other kingdom known to man. Unfortunately, many people who proclaim citizenship do not access the benefits. Even when you abide by the Kingdom laws as a principle, you can tap into some level of success, but you can reach insurmountable heights when you align with the laws from a heart of intimacy in demonstration as a lifestyle.

The Kingdom laws are extremely peculiar. Where human laws are created to contain and restrict, Heaven's laws expand and free. Where earth's rulers are encouraging depopulation in preparation for lack and depleting resources, Heaven is mandating citizens to multiply with inexhaustible resources as a supply. Where earth's rulers are paying more, researching more, and achieving depleting results with healthcare, Heaven's healthcare policy is complete; no payments, no doctors, no hospital stay, no treatments, but rather a cure. The laws simply place you in the position to catch the blessings being thrown to you.

Kingdom of Heaven resources

Some economies are built on crude oil, some on gold, some on diamonds, and still yet others on technology, the kingdom of YHWH is not different; it also has resources. The Kingdom of Heaven exports to Earth all of its resources; physical and spiritual. In Heaven, life begins and ends. No Kingdom has the power or authority to create life as the Kingdom of Heaven does. Heaven imports every life: plant, animal, people, and spirit life. When something is needed on the Earth, Heaven must fill the order. Heaven creates every molecule that composes the Earth's matter and replenishes every resource that supplies life's wants and needs. Heaven provides every resource even down to the oxygen flow of the Earth. Heaven is the only provider of inexhaustible resources, and orders have always been filled freely.

Portals of supply and protection are closed for those who deny Heaven as the source. For this reason, the Earth has experienced tragic disasters, winds of drought, famine, floods, and intense frosts as consequences for rebellion against YHWH. When a person chooses to close the doors to righteousness, they open the doors to the reign of the rulers of Hell.

Science and the media are major proponents of spread arguments about global warming or overpopulation. Lack or depletion are erroneous thoughts to Kingdom citizens because they know their King provided enough space and resources for every life that He has sent here. The resources of Heaven are eternally inexhaustible, and no economy on the earth can boast or compare.

In the book of Matthew, Yeshua gave the parable of a wicked man. The man owed a lot of money (ten thousand bags of gold or more than 20 years of work) to the king. The king requested that the man sell himself, his wife, his children, and all of his possessions to repay the debt. The man pleaded with the king on his knees, the king felt pity, and he decided to cancel his debt. Later the man saw a fellow servant who owed money (100 days of labor) to him, and rather than canceling his debt as a thanksgiving for what the king had done for him, the man jumped on his fellow servant, choked him, demanded payback, and had him thrown into prison. Onlookers saw what happened and reported back to the master. Accordingly, the king said, "You wicked man!", and ordered him to be tortured, and put in prison.

Similarly, YHWH appointed earthly governments as recipients of favor from the King. They receive heavenly imports: some by grace and some on the basis of submission to Heaven. The Earth's governments have passed down blessings and curses to their people. Unlike other kingdoms, Heaven only passes on blessings. The King has and always will dethrone kingdoms who wickedly supply to their citizens when they have received abundantly. He will also justify those who have committed evil against His citizens. A great shaking of rebellious kings is coming!

Prepare For Colonization

When colonization occurs, so does war. For expanding kingdoms with historic prestige such as King Nebuchadnezzar when he was expanding the Babylonian empire, or Alexander the Great when he was expanding the Greek empire; they all experienced war as they would increase the reach of their borders and change the allegiance of their new citizens. The rulers of the previous kingdom would be dethroned and new supervision declared.

As a kingdom of Heaven ambassador, you have been mandated to colonize the Earth. The kingdom in darkness will fight as you remove the borders of Heaven, and bring the Earth back to its created intent.

Just as military personnel train to prepare for battle, you should be training in good and bad. Stay armed. In the battle, you never complete your education. I am not making reference of institutional education, but rather revelation that is given from eternal light sources. You MUST keep seeking YHWH, learning, and updating yourself, so you can win the war. As new technology and intelligence is given, militaries all over the Earth go into training to stay current on the use of new weapons and new opponent strategies; you are no different in YHWH's kingdom!

Ignorance is the primary reason people fail in their life assignments. Punishment is assigned to the ignorant and those who are intentionally defiant. They are both sent for eternal judgment. If you did not know before reading this book, today, you understand some of the requirements as a Kingdom of Heaven Ambassador, and as we continue, you will understand even more. One mission-essential requirement for a Kingdom of Heaven Ambassador is to flee from ignorance by being intentional in training. There are many areas you will need to train in. You want to be as full of the ability to apply knowledge as possible, so the enemy's efforts are neutralized and unsuccessful. I want to discuss with you two primary areas that you MUST do continual training:

1. Repentance

When the September 11th tragedy took place on American soil, when the twin tours were hit, and over 3,000 people killed, Dr. Condoleezza Rice was the US Secretary of State. She describes the sense of regret and guilt she felt knowing that the country's most classified intelligence was given to her in order that she could exercise her authority by creating a strategy for protecting the nation's citizens. Unfortunately, the attack already happened, and there is nothing that can be done about it now. The tragedy brought increased attention to the prevalence of opposition to the American norm, the possible strategies that could have deterred the event, and how other countries can avoid a similar circumstance.

Similarly, you will learn things that are within your power to change in order to be the greatest asset to yourself, your descendants, and the world populace. To repent is like doing a "U" turn. It simply means to become aware of a wrong approach, to ask forgiveness from YHWH, and to change. As a result of your birth into sin and your gradual learning process, you are now and you will in the future identify habits, thoughts, attitudes, and associations you will have to remove to maintain the integrity of your relationship with YHWH and your potential as a vehicle for Kingdom growth. YHWH sees the suffering of his creation; that's why you are here. Do not suffer or let other people suffer on your watch because you have been bestowed with the tools and access for them to experience otherwise.

The capabilities of the Earth's governments to protect are far limited in comparison to Heaven. No breaches happen in Heaven, and with your access, and their repentance, that benefit can be afforded to Earth's kingdoms. The catastrophic news we hear will be an object of history for those kingdoms who align with Heaven. In order for you to activate this liberation in yourself or in others, you must first make a strategy to change your current approach. People are suffering, and you hold the keys to their answer. Will you open the door for your liberty and the liberty of others, or will you stay in bondage to, Satan, the most vicious and deceitful ruler of all time? Whether you knew it before or not, the Bible tells us the options are two: yield to the Kingdom of Heaven or the kingdom in darkness. Reading this may be your first revelation of your role in the Kingdom, and we have just begun to scratch the surface. I want to stop and lead you into a prayer now to release you into the fullness of being a Kingdom of Heaven Ambassador. Say this aloud:

Father, I have come to a deeper realization of your majesty, your power, your glory, and your design for my life. I confess that I have fallen short of your assignment for me on this Earth, and I now understand what Yeshua did for me when He died on the cross and rose again. I believe that Yeshua rose, and I thank you for the resurrection power that you have given me. I declare that from today on, I will exercise my authority as your ambassador on this Earth. I invite your Kingdom to come in every area of my life, and I submit myself as your vessel to advance your Kingdom thru the Earth. I vow to crucify my flesh daily and instead to walk in Your divine order. Provide for me this day everything that I need to succeed in my assignment. I loose from captivity everyone who I hold hostage in unforgiveness, and I request that you cleanse me from all evil: cancel demonic activity, cancel curses, and resurrect any dead areas of my life. Lead me closer to you, and guide me away from evil in Yeshua' name. Amen.

When you identify something in you that is defiant, rebellious, or otherwise opposite of YHWH's will, repent. Repent for holding people hostage thru unforgiveness, repent for making a god in your image rather than believing YHWH is His own, repent for lust of the heart or the flesh, remove pride, and all other evils. Many things will present themselves as you pursue your life journey. Make repentance a continual area of training, crucify your will, and prepare for things that hinder your assignment to be pruned.

2. Multiplication

Before a person dies, their last words are arguably the most honored words that they may have spoken. Similarly, I cherish Yeshua' last words, and I recommend that you do too! Before

Yeshua ascended, his last words to his disciples are our colonization mandate. He said:

"All authority in heaven and on earth has been given to me. Therefore go and make disciples of all nations, baptizing them in the name of the Father and of the Son and of the Holy Spirit, and teaching them to obey everything I have commanded you. And surely I am with you always, to the very end of the age."

He was telling you exactly what to multiply in others: spiritual baptism (immersion into the nature of Father, the son, and the Holy Spirit), his teaching, his deeds and disciple-making. Be intentional in growing your intimacy with YHWH and your ability to multiply the impact of His love thru making disciples of others. With the current information highways, there are now more than ever many ways to disciple and multiply. You are supposed to train in the word of Righteousness until you become a soldier who rightly divides the word of truth and are prepared for every good work. (See Hebrews 5:13, 2 Tim. 2:15, 2 Tim. 2:21) Multiply your skill and disciples for the Kingdom!

CHAPTER TWO

TAKE POSSESSION OF WHAT'S YOURS

From the days of John the Baptist until now the kingdom of heaven has suffered violence, and the violent take it by force.
-Matthew 11:12

The Story Of Abram

When Abram was born (later to be renamed Abraham by YHWH), wickedness was rampant on the Earth. Nimrod (a mighty warrior) ruled the Earth and its inhabitants. He was more wicked than all of the men that lived from the time of the flood onward. He worshipped other gods, consulted sorcerers, and engaged in other forms of witchcraft. Terah (Abram's father) was well taken care of in the kingdom of Nimrod because his father, Nahor, was a prince in his court. When Abram was born, a sign showed in the Heavens. A star from the East came and swallowed four other stars. With the actions of the stars, wise men of that time interpreted the sign that Abram would bear nations that would devour other nations and rule. Accordingly, when Nimrod found out, he decided to kill Abram, but his father outsmarted him, and he was spared.

Satan is aware of your assignment

When Abram was born, people were able to tap into supernatural power illegally to gain insight. They had an understanding of the stars and were able to use them to discern a baby was a threat. A similar situation occurred when Yeshua was born. The stars foretold his birth and King Herod (Satan's instrument) mandated all of the newborn babies be killed to prevent the manifestation of YHWH's plan.

Today, Satan is still scouting to stay aware of what is going on in his enemy's camp, and you are included in his intelligence. He is looking for your weaknesses, your errors, and your vulnerabilities. In Judy Coventry's book, *Trading Floors*, she said Sin has intellectual property. When you use the intellectual property of Sin--lies, cheating, slander, hatred, immoral behavior, witchcraft, etc., you are exercising a licensing agreement; each use is charged. Liens are placed on your blessings even to the point of shortening your lifespan, and plaguing your descendants.

The Fall Of Satan and his fallen Angels

The prophet Ezekial told us about the fall of Satan in Ezekial 28. It tells us Lucifer (his name before the fall) was a covering cherub before the throne of YHWH. His job was to reflect the light of YHWH and to create an atmosphere of worship for YHWH. In the midst of his assignment, he began to orchestrate evil thoughts, and the Bible says he fell because of "unrighteous trade".

The center of every economy is the trading floors. Similar to America's Wall Street trading floors, every countries' trading floors orchestrate the trade of currency and assets. Investors go to the trading floor to buy or sell goods.

Similarly, the Kingdom of Heaven also has trading floors. Satan and the fallen angels have been found guilty of unrighteous trading, and have been thrown out of Heaven with the verdict of eternal suffering in Sheol. Unlike you, they do not have a chance at redemption because the blood of Yeshua paid the price for those with blood, unlike the angels who have light flowing thru them rather than blood.

Ezekial 28:17 says, "Your heart was proud because of your beauty; you corrupted your wisdom for the sake of your splendor." With this scripture, we know Lucifer exchanged his beauty for pride, and wisdom for splendor. He took compliments and began to amass a proud confidence he could be like YHWH. The light of YHWH which provides insight and discloses the plans of YHWH, Satan chose to exchange for unrighteous attention. He was to reflect the light and plans of YHWH with the stones that adorned his body, so that Heaven's inhabitants can walk in the plans of YHWH. He had insight of man's role in the plans of YHWH, and he desired prestige for himself. He wanted to slight YHWH and attempt to dethrone Him. As he traded unrighteously, he took from the supply of others to increase his own opulence. As a result, YHWH ordered him to be thrown out of Heaven.

Genesis 6 tells us about the time of Noah where some of Heaven's angels fell. It tells us that the angels saw the woman were beautiful, they chose to marry some of them, and contaminated the seed of man creating a race of "nephilim". The fallen angels traded the insight of Heaven for prestige; aside from the authorization of YHWH, and wickedness increased on the Earth. They told things they were not supposed to tell in exchange for allegiance and to win prestige. Today, Satan and the fallen angels still attempt to contaminate the seed, win souls, and partake of the inheritance of man. Yeshua told us that the end times will be like the times of Noah: genetic tampering, increasing wickedness, and favor of the elect. Be vigilant!

Take Back Your Seed!

Satan was adorned with 9 stones: carnelian, chrysolite, and moonstone, beryl, onyx, and jasper, sapphire, turquoise, and emerald (Ezekial 28:13). In E.W. Bullinger's book, *Number in Scripture*, it tells us many details about biblical numerology. The number 9 is the number for finality and judgement. The Bible tells us Lucifer was created perfect, but because of his choices, he was thrown out of Heaven as a portion of his judgement. Ezekial 28:12 says, "You were the signet of perfection, full of wisdom and perfect in beauty."

The priests of YHWH were commanded to adorn themselves with 12 stones: Exodus 28:17-21 says:

You shall set in it four rows of stones. A row of carnelian, chrysolite, and emerald shall be the first row; and the second row a turquoise, a sapphire, and a moonstone; and the third row a jacinth, an agate, and an amethyst; and the fourth row a beryl, an onyx, and a jasper; they shall be set in gold filigree. There shall be twelve stones with names corresponding to the names of the sons of Israel; they shall be like signets, each engraved with its name, for the twelve tribes.

You were created to fill the role of ambassador and priest. You are an heir of the eternal Kingdom. 1 Peter 2:4 says, "Come to him, a living stone, though rejected by mortals yet chosen and precious in YHWH's sight, and 5 like living stones, let yourselves be built into a spiritual house, to be a holy priesthood, to offer spiritual sacrifices acceptable to YHWH through Yeshua the Messiah. " The attributes that distinguish each of the twelve tribes can be found in Yeshua, and following him, you contain the attributes as well.

The number 12, is a number that reflects perfection of governmental foundation. E.W. Bullinger said:

"TWELVE is a perfect number, signifying perfection of government, or of governmental perfection. It is found as a multiple in all that has to do with rule. The sun which "rules" the day, and the moon and stars which "govern" the night, do so by their passage through the twelve signs of the Zodiac which completes the great circle of the heavens of 360 (12 x 30) degrees or divisions, and thus govern the year. Twelve is the product of 3 (the perfectly Divine and heavenly number) and 4 (the earthly, the number of what is material and organic). While seven is composed of 3 added to 4, twelve is 3 multiplied by 4, and hence denotes that which can scarcely be explained in words, but which the spiritual perception can at once appreciate."

From the time of Adam and Eve, Satan has attempted to devour the seed that inherits the Kingdom of Heaven. He and the fallen angels were not created to fulfill governmental assignments. He was created to reflect the image of YHWH in perfection and judgement, but he desires to fulfill the governmental role of man as the heir of Heaven. He is jealous and deficient, immoral and illegal, a thief, murderer, and theft. He does not have all of the necessary ingredients to administer the Kingdom of Heaven and YHWH knew this when He created him. Satan does not have all of the necessities to govern your territory; accordingly, YHWH has assigned you to do it. He attempts to trade unrighteousness for your inheritance, and you are fully equipped to overthrow him and take your inheritance back.

You have been granted back your inheritance in the Messiah, but that does not automatically mean you possess it. The land of Canaan was given to Abraham and to his children by an eternal inheritance, but it was not until many years later before they even stepped their foot on it.

Your land has been liberated from the hand of the enemy by the sacrifice of Yeshua the Messiah, but you have to take the land like the Israelites physically took the land of Canaan. It might even shock you to know that even after Yeshua has liberated your territory, Satan still occupies it because you have not removed him. However, his occupation is illegal. So what you need do is guerilla warfare to expel him and to fully settle in your land. He is an illegal occupant; and unless you fight, he will not give up the territory even though it has been legally liberated from his control. He is a rebel and will always be. So take the name of Yeshua and the Sword of the Spirit, praying with all manners of prayer and liberate your land from the hand of the enemy.

Satan continuously fights to steal your joy, your peace, your property, your sanctity. Satan has already been defeated, but he resents giving up control until you take it by force. His occupation is illegal; get him out of your territory. Get him out of the region of Peace in your territory, chase him out of the northern border of Joy in your territory, hoist the banner of victory over the city called Property in your territory; kick him out of your farmlands of Sanctity in the name of Yeshua. He has no right whatsoever to steal your joy, peace, property and sanctity. The ground he has is the one you have permitted him to take. Kick him out!

Facing The Truth Of Persecution For Firm Standing In Yeshua

Paul had to make a choice to return to Caiaphas (the priest that handed Yeshua to Pilate for blasphemy) face the possibility of death, and express to him he had become a traitor in his court. Peter had the choice to abandon the message of Yeshua or be crucified upside down on the cross. John had the choice to dilute his message or be stranded alone on the Island of Patmos. Stephen had a choice to conceal his witness of Yeshua or be stoned to death. You also have a choice. You must decide, will you un-apologetically share your witness of Yeshua even when you're faced with brutality?

Simply for standing firm, Christians throughout the centuries have experienced an increasing amount of persecution. Christian Today has estimated that 70 million Christians have been killed in the 2000 years since Yeshua walked the Earth; simply for their witness.

Kingdom of Heaven citizens stick out like a "sore thumb"! They are on a different calendar, dependent on a different economy, moving to a different light speed, defiant of the status quo, and willing to sacrifice all for their King to be pleased. We are obvious and we should be! Our kingdom is beyond this arena!

Yeshua used salt as a metaphor to describe our assignment on the Earth. Salt is used to clean, kill bacteria, disinfect, add flavor, melt, preserve, stabilize, polish, revitalize, restore, medicate, deodorize, brighten, revive, speed, enhance circulation, and recolor; amongst other uses.

The book of Enoch says in the chamber of the lightning, each lightning represents a righteous person. We are to be bold, pungent, distinguished, and definitive! We can bring awe, honor, holy fear, and humility all with one stroke. We are a gate that opens the door of life and closes the door to death; a very delicate passageway. We comply with Yeshua in the face of opposition knowing that even if everything is taken in this realm, everything is gained in Heaven. For this reason, Yeshua said:

"Blessed are those who are persecuted for righteousness' sake, for theirs is the kingdom of heaven. Blessed are you when people revile you and persecute you and utter all kinds of evil against you falsely on my account. Rejoice and be glad, for your reward is great in heaven, for in the same way they persecuted the prophets who were before you.

We have been mandated by Yeshua to colonize the Earth, take the territory back from Satan, and keep moving the borders until all of the Earth is overtaken by the Kingdom of Heaven. We are mandated to multiply prolifically! Colonization comes with war!

When Britain went to Africa to find slaves as laborers for the "New World", they came to an established land. The African people had families, businesses, responsibilities, religions, cultural mannerisms, hierarchies were in place, and people had plans. Families were separated, businesses were abandoned, responsibilities were transferred, religions were desecrated, and people acted defiantly.

When the Americas were colonized, inhabitants had pre-established ways. Religions, taxes, customs, holidays, and responsibilities were imposed. People were not willing to make changes or adjustments willingly and war too place.

Similarly, the land you will be colonizing is pre-occupied by the kingdom of darkness. They have settled in and made comfortable homes, customs, ways, and mannerisms. They have no intent to willingly depart from the property, but it has been purchased by Yeshua and is their illegally occupied residence. Accordingly, you have been assigned as the ambassador to provide eviction notices.

When we stand in our definitive position; un-apologetically for Yeshua, we shine light on strongholds of the kingdom of darkness. They have invested thousands of years to build some of the walls and thicken the chains they have placed on the people you will see. We are removing them from our property and freeing their slaves. They want to contaminate your seed, take your inheritance, and overthrow the plans of YHWH, so when you polish, disinfect, melt, deodorize, revitalize, or restore (as the salt is assigned to do), you will run into a fight. You're polishing areas that they have stained and melting structures that they have welded, so what do you expect?

You may have to introduce families with established occult traditions to the truth of their ways. You may have to reject meals and gifts. You may have to look a person in the eyes and introduce them to the reality that what they are saying is not true, and when you do, you may not be received with hugs and kisses. You may have to preach to a congregation of defiant people. Dependent on their position of authority, you may receive slander and you may receive the judgement to be beheaded. Will you be able to stand in the truth despite the cost?

Many people read the story of Jonah and the whale as a children's fairytale, but it is a historic truth. Jonah was instructed by YHWH to go to a land that was wicked and tell them YHWH would be judging them. Jonah 1:1 says:

Now the word of the Lord came to Jonah son of Amittai, saying, "Go at once to Nineveh, that great city, and cry out against it; for their wickedness has come up before me."

In other kingdoms that received similar verdicts as Ninevah (such as Sodom and Gomorrah or Babel), many brutal deaths had occurred, rape and molestation were norms, robbery was legal, adultery was traditional, and mistreating people was praised. Jonah, being a man of YHWH, would have been well-informed about wicked behavior, and he would have been able to suspect that going to Ninevah while they are in such an uproar of defiance could be dangerous. He probably was well aware his message could cause extreme torture, humiliation, and the end of his life.

After being transported unwillingly in the mouth of the whale, he had to choose to speak the message of YHWH despite the consequences, and without physical defense. He was in a wicked land by himself. That's asking for trouble!

Imagine going to one of the areas in America with the worse crime rates. Imagine taking a ship to get there and being on foot or making arrangements to rent or buy an animal for transportation. Even worse, imagine being instructed to go to a place that is so bad YHWH himself is going to wipe them out. It's not safe. You could be robbed. You could be molested or raped. You could be skinned. The possibilities are endless when the populace has reached those extremes of wicked behavior, and in historic instances, the wickedness is so common it is legal! At a time where you do not have a quick physical route to exit and no physical army for defense, would you go?

Your position may be similar to Jonah's today or in the future. We are in the end times where evil is increasing. When a wound is very open, salt burns very bad. Similarly, your role will be very apparent and sometimes painful for others as recipient of the truth, but you cannot dilute the message! Speak the truth regardless of the cost!

Some had to face death. Some had to face slander. Some sat in prison cells. Some lost limbs. Some had to see their reputations butchered. Some had to be rejected by their closest loved ones. You do not know the price you will have to pay, but you must stand on the truth regardless. Will you stand in courage and follow Yeshua regardless of the cost?

My challenge to you:

- Write down ways or areas you have been convicted about your tolerance

- Repent for being tolerant and commit to aligning with Yeshua

Repeat this vow that changed my life:

Yeshua, I repent for every instance where I have not fulfilled the role that you have assigned me as the salt and light of the Earth. Forgive me and cleanse me with your blood. I place your blood over every circumstance that flashed thru my memory right now -- where I have not walked into the pungent and definitive role that you have assigned me. I vow to you this day that I will fulfill your colonization mandate and bring the Kingdom of Heaven onto this Earth. I present myself to you today as a living sacrifice. I stand willing to speak the truth regardless of the cost; understanding that your grace is more than sufficient for me to transcend this realm. I vow to fulfill the assignment you have given me as a Kingdom of Heaven ambassador today and forevermore. Amen.

When something is in his control, it has signs

I once heard a man of YHWH say: if the Holy Spirit comes to town in a red suit and a bola hat, can you recognize Him? Well, I know the Holy Spirit by the works that accompany His presence, I know Him by the fruits that His presence produces. In the same way, I know the devil when I see him, I know the devil by his works and fruits, I know the devil when I see him:

Sickness. Sickness is of the devil, a child of the devil and an enemy of YHWH and man. When I see one, call it whatever name, I see the devil. It is his fruit and it is his work.

Shame. Again, when I see shame, I see the devil at work at his best. The worst thing that can happen to a person is to be bowed down in shame and rejection. Today, 70 to 90 percent of the youth of our nations are down with shame, guilt and rejection all because of the cloud of sin hanging over their spirits. It started with their father Adam; when he sinned against YHWH in the garden, he discovered first of all He was naked; he was ashamed and went to hide himself from the presence of YHWH. So shame still is of the devil, and when I see it, I see the devil at work.

Guilt. Nothing is as crippling and satanic as guilt-it is the strongest force of the devil. When Satan gets one down in it, then that person is doomed for life. This is because, the only person YHWH cannot help is the person ridden and bowed down completely with guilt, so unless you rid yourself of guilt through the word of YHWH and by the verbal application of the blood of Yeshua, then you are in the devil's stronghold for life. When I see guilt, I see the devil.

Suffering. If there is anything that devil wants and wishes on humanity, it is suffering. He takes pride in seeing YHWH's love suffer. It is his way of getting at YHWH, it is like saying to YHWH, I know I cannot get you but I will get to your children and give them untold suffering, by so doing YHWH, I am indirectly getting to you. When I see suffering, I see Satan's wickedness and callousness.

The fruits of the flesh. The flesh is enticed by the works of

Satan when it is weak. The flesh cannot be tamed, it cannot be calmed or trained. It simply must be crucified. Daily, hourly, and at even greater frequencies, we must choose to present our choices, our will, our imagination, and our emotions to the control of Yeshua. The flesh speaks to us is first person; intriguing us with concepts that idolize self. Everything that comes from allowing the flesh to govern is evil and satanic. From the day man fell in Eden, his flesh became corrupt and from that day till now it has become the house of the devil to carry out his perverseness and evil passions. In Galatians 5:19-21, Paul the Apostle gave us a list of the acts of the devil working through the flesh. It says:

Now the works of the flesh are obvious: fornication, impurity, licentiousness, idolatry, sorcery, enmities, strife, jealousy, anger, quarrels, dissensions, factions, envy, drunkenness, carousing, and things like these.

When Satan has authority to something, it is unauthorized, and illegal. Redemption stripped Satan of all and any authority he has over the human race. The only thing left in his hand is ignorance and darkness. If he rules in a place, it is because darkness and ignorance dominates there, he knows his reign is illegal so he goes hiding to rule where people do not know his reign has been truncated by Him who died and rose again from the dead on the third day.

So that today, whatever and wherever he has the dominion, it is because the people don't know; he is therefore unauthorized and illegal. He is a fake and a fad.

With the blood of Yeshua, you can take your territory back from him and send him running. We have an atomic weapon that can ruin the complete arsenal of the evil one with one detonation; it is the blood of Yeshua. With it all the artilleries in his arsenal are brought to ruin if directed on target. The blood of Yeshua, verbally proclaimed or pled will bring down the devil's strongest hold and liberate the believer's territory in a moment of time -- keeping the devil on the run.

We have said earlier there can be no complete redemption, if the place and position of man before the fall is not restored back to him. Man did not fall from heaven; he fell from dominion over the earth, and redemption is such that he can be brought back to the place of dominion as before the fall.

The Webster's 1828 dictionary defines dominion thus: Sovereign or supreme authority; the power of governing and controlling, power to direct, control, use and dispose of at pleasure and right of governing. So to dominate for short is to have the right to govern.

The believer has the right to govern situations, circumstance, devils, bodies, animate and inanimate objects, and that right is in the name of Yeshua and through the power of the spoken word.

Adam ruled creation by the word of his power, the same way YHWH rules creation and the entire universe. Yeshua came as the example of the man of YHWH and showed us how Adam did it or should have done it (in his 3½ years of ministry.) Then he died and changed roles, came back by His Spirit to dwell with us and to continue what He started. When we carefully examined the four gospels, we will see how Yeshua did it, how He took and exercised the Adamic dominion.

Thru the payment of Yeshua, you have been granted dominion

Man's dominion or ruler-ship was lost to the devil at the fall and until a price was paid to make for the sin of man, he could not have his "right of governing" back. When Yeshua hung there on the cross some two thousand years ago and cried: IT IS FINISHED. As our priest, he is now seated at the right hand of the Father. In the Old Testament, the priest was never permitted to sit in the presence of YHWH because his work of atonement thru animal blood sacrifice was never complete. He had to return annually to atone for the people; standing in the presence of YHWH. Now, Yeshua, the Lord of rest, the Lord of the Sabbath, is seated in a position of rest because His sacrifice atoned for us eternally. This means everything that has robbed you of your right of governing has been taken care of, that which has stopped you from being who you were created to be has been fixed, now you can come back home to your place of ruler-ship.

The payment of the ransom YHWH demands-BLOOD was made by the Messiah on the behalf of the human race and now all who believes can be saved, restored back to YHWH in grace, power and to their rightful position as sons and daughters of YHWH with right of governing. That was why Yeshua died, that is why your access back to the garden of dominion is granted back. Come back home.

Access to assign the angels

Are they not all ministering spirits sent forth to minister for those who shall be heirs of salvation? (Hebrews 1:14). Yes, they are. Your right of governing reaches to the realm of angels. Paul said that even the believer will judge angels at the end of time. (See 1 Cor. 6:3). We have in the program of YHWH as it relates to rights of governing, the authority to give orders to angels.

They are given charge by YHWH to obey and to carry out our orders in so far as those orders are in line with the word of YHWH. Please note the angels do not carry out unholy and selfish orders, but they are obliged to do the will of YHWH that we speak in response to moving of the Holy Spirit per time in our lives. (See Psalm 103:20) Angels answer to the Sword of the Spirit in your mouth.

Dominion over your health

Yeshua in his atoning sacrifice, paid and suffered duly for every sickness and every disease the world has ever known and by his resurrection from the dead, He declared sicknesses and diseases illegal. He ended the reign of diseases and truncated the dominion of sicknesses and in their place; you were exalted to the place of honor and ruler-ship.

Sicknesses and diseases are under your feet; with the word of your mouth, with the word of your power, you have the dominion over your body and your health. (See Eccl. 8:4).

Dominion over time, nature, the land, and the animals

YHWH's original intent was that Adam rule through his word, creatures in the sky, creatures on the earth and creatures in the water, His plan and program has not changed; by redemption it has even become more encompassing. The new creation man has dominion over the land and animals. I know of a man of YHWH who through the spoken word, ruled fishes in the water and even his land. He was a farmer and by the spoken word dominated the soil of his land and causes it to always yield its increase.

These things hear the voice of the word of the Lord in our mouth. I personally speak to everything in my house and they hear me. I remember some years ago when I first moved into my present apartment, everything I touched in the apartment, was falling apart and getting spoiled in my hands, then one day the Holy Spirit inspired me to start talking to the things in my house and that they will hear me; I did and today, I tell you, everything in my house hears my voice and they obey me. Nothing just goes bad in my house, until I release them to go. We rule creation by the word of YHWH spoken through our mouths.

Dominion over your finances

Money is a spirit, it has intelligence; it has ears, eyes and can talk. We have dominion over our finances by the spoken word. When a man does his part of giving and then continues to speak to his finances, money will grow wings and come to that person in the name of the Lord. Money has ears, it is an angel, and it is subject to the name of Yeshua. I have had in my life a miraculous supply of finances that I cannot explain. I have received deposits in my bank accounts several times without knowing who made the deposits.

Nobody ever called me to say I have deposited money into your account, pastor, but the money just keeps coming in. I know the secret and I am doing it-giving and speaking to my finances. Money is under my feet.

Dominion over your thoughts

We are what we think; nobody ever rises above his thoughts and words, but the good news is that we have authority, right of governing over our thoughts. Thoughts are strong weapons in the hand of the enemy; he uses them against us most of time, holding us in captivity. He does fire arrows of dirty, limiting, filthy and weak thoughts into our minds, but we can take every thought captive to the obedience of the Messiah through the Sword of the Spirit in the name of Yeshua. (See 2 Cor. 10: 5) As a person thinks in his heart so is he. (See Proverbs 23:7)

Dominion over your attitudes

An intelligent mind once said: your attitude, determines your altitude. How true! Attitudes are the disposition or the state of mind of a person; it can be negative or positive. When it is negative, it can be more destructive than Satan himself but when it is positive, it is power, a force to be reckoned with on the earth.

Now, it would suffice us to know we can control our attitude; we can align them with YHWH's word and bring it under subjection to the Holy Spirit of YHWH. You can speak to your attitude and it can be brought into captivity to the obedience of the Messiah. No genuine and sincere believer should have attitudinal problems. Cut your attitude to shape and size through the Sword of the Spirit.

Dominion over your actions

Our actions speak volumes about who we really are, I know a person not just by what he says but by what he does. Some people are sweet tongued but poor doers, so by ones actions he or she can be justified. The good thing is we are restored to dominion over our actions. There is a fruit of the spirit called self-control, that relates to our action. So by the Holy Spirit and His Sword in our mouths, we can have the dominion over our actions. There is this confession I make in my place of prayer every morning: "Today, I speak and behave myself wisely, all my actions and negotiations are done in wisdom, in the spirit of love and humility in the name of Yeshua." That way, I control my actions for the day.

You should be making disciples that do the same

YHWH takes pride in seeing us take our place in the body and recover our territories from the hand of the devil, but He derives pleasure much more when we become His instrument of liberation to others. We are saved to save others, we are called to call others; we are liberated to liberate others. We are part of YHWH's redemptive program, Yeshua undertook the ultimate part, we continue on to the completion of the work until everyone has been told the story and everyone has been liberated. Freed, now go set others free, a follower of the Messiah, now go make other followers. In this shall you be my disciple, if you do what I say. (See John 15:8)

CHAPTER THREE

DIVORCE THE DEVIL

Have you seen the family that attends church every time the doors open? Their kids do all of their assignments from children's church. The parents appear to be happy in their marriage, and they do their best to live righteously. Despite it all, their house has been broken into, they have always struggled financially, and they do not seem to have many unnecessary expenses. Have you seen them?

Have you wondered, "Why does this family have it so hard, and it seems they are doing things right?" Have you ever thought maybe they might be in a marriage covenant with the devil, and they might not even know it? This scenario is true of many people in church (properly translated from the Greek word "ekklesia" as a set apart assembly). The marriage contract with Satan has steadily increased in demands over the years. It has moved so slowly and generationally most people have not observed their true allegiance, neither do they know that an allegiance with him is there.

Churches are busy teaching spiritual warfare without realizing many people are actually only having couple spats with the devil. They say, "Devil, get out of my finances", but will lay in the same bed with him when it gives them a raise at their job. They need to break the covenant!

Our world history is infiltrated with pagan worship and defiance from the fall of man on. Variances of customs, traditions, religions, practices, and tendencies have marked Satan's bride and shown her commitment to the marriage covenant. He has lusted over the beauty of the bride of Yahshua for centuries and attempted to defile her by introducing her to his ways and influencing her to pursue them. In history, we can see he led the Babylonian empire, the Egyptian empire, Sodom and Gomorrah, the Greek empire, the Roman Empire, and we can see their influences and adaptation in the world's prevailing kingdoms today.

The greatest deception for the Christian church finds its roots in the reign of Rome; where the statues, the holidays, the calendar, and the customs merged so much people today believe their ways have biblical origins that in truth they do not. In this way, because your attention, sacrifices, and affection is misdirected for the sake of apostasy, Satan has deceitfully won your worship.

The laws of YHWH are more than rules. They are your marriage covenant with the Son of God. The church is the bride of Yahshua. You are the bride of Yahshua.

Every marriage has a discussion between the husband and the wife before the covenant is entered where they discuss what is acceptable. Things like how often the wife cooks, chores, holidays, religions, special days, attire, and proper and improper treatment are discussed.

When I met my husband, we courted daily. We would discuss a topic and lay out both views on the topic. He would say his perspective. I would say my perspective. We would both read the biblical perspective, and we married our perspectives to YHWH's in our courting process. We discussed how we talk to one another, dress and grooming that is attractive to one another's taste, how we pick friends, people we keep around us, how many kids we want, how we want to raise our kids, and many other topics. When we got married, we both knew we were agreeing, not just to words with our mouths, but to the compromise of our ways. I could no longer display ways that were not subjected to the opinion of my husband and authority of YHWH, and he could no longer display ways that were not subjected to my opinion and YHWH's authority. I could not do my hair, dress, pick my friends, or eat food that is not subjected to his authority, and neither could he do these things without subjecting his authority to YHWH. The marriage covenant is a complete metamorphosis that teaches me selflessness and how to be a submitted vessel to YHWH every day.

In your marriage contract with Yeshua, He has given similar statutes to abide by. He has said what to wear, who to keep in your company, how to act, how to romance him, and when he will abandon you. He said you shall have no other gods (husbands) except him. He tells you what special days He desires to spend with you, what special meals he likes to eat with you, what is His idea of romance, how He likes intimacy with you, and the list goes on. The Bible is supposed to be read as your manual for intimacy with Yeshua. You take the manual and live the life of intimacy with His letter to you as the basis.

On the contrary, many people who call themselves a part of the bride of Yahshua have taken His love letters and read them, some store them, some idolize them, and they have not exercised the advice in them as a lifestyle. They are His personal advice to you. The Bible is not a god, and it cannot be honored higher than YHWH. It is simply a document listing his desires for you.

When my husband and I met, he would write me letters daily, and I would write letters to him. When we were apart, we would read the letters to refresh our memories of our togetherness. The letters seemed to rekindle the memory and the intimacy of our relationship. They motivated us during the immigration process because we both would read the letters and remember how great a time that we had together. When we were separated, we had to pay for phone time because we were in different countries. We had to do visas simply to see one another, and the flights were very costly. We were well aware there were many physical and financial barriers preventing us from being together, but when we would read the letters, the spirit behind the letter was kindled, and we could glimpse at togetherness again.

Similarly, Yeshua walked amongst mankind physically 2000 years ago. Since, only few are invested enough to see him today. At the time, his bride was married to another man (the devil). She had honored and cherished his ways so much she defended her husband to witness his death. She stood silent. She mourned, but she did not contend.

Today, the mark of the covenant with Satan is still readily obvious. His calendar, his holy days, his customs, and his sacrifices have become deeply rooted into our being and we are intertwined with them as a man is intertwined with his wife in the marriage bed. We must divorce him and run back to our first love (as was foretold by John to the Laodicea church in Revelations), but we first must make note of the symbols of our covenant with him.

The symbols

Many of the symbols we see and use everyday are symbols of our covenant with Satan that began during the times of Noah. They can be seen in our homes, in our appearance, and in our ways. Truth is hidden like a mustard seed in a forest. The end times are here, so the symbols are common and no longer offensive, but you must divorce them or subject yourself to the judgment of wearing the mark of the beast. Regarding our times, Yeshua said:

For as the days of Noah were, so will be the coming of the Son of Man. For as in those days before the flood they were eating and drinking, marrying and giving in marriage, until the day Noah entered the ark, and they knew nothing until the flood came and swept them all away, so too will be the coming of the Son of Man. (Matthew 24:38-39)

The great grandson of Noah was Nimrod. Nimrod was born on the day the sun is reborn, the winter solstice, which typically falls on December 25th. The book of Jasher tells us that he was a great warrior, his expert military skills stimulated his rule of the world. He became the king of the whole world. He was married to a woman named Semiramis. Nimrod was the king who authorized the building of the tower of Babel and who built Ninevah. He was well known for idolatry, drunkenness, and deception in his leadership.

When Nimrod died, the people deified him. He was the first person to be epitomized as a god. They said he ascended and became the sun.

After his death, legends say the rays of the sun impregnated his wife, Semiramis, and she became pregnant with a son named, Tammuz. Tammuz took the place of his dad in ruling the kingdom. He and his mom were known to have an intimate relationship. He was a mighty hunter, but in his 40th year, he was killed by a wild boar.

You are probably wondering, "What does this story have to do with anything?" The Bible tells us Satan has some foreknowledge of the plans of YHWH. He knows some things before their time. Accordingly, he introduces deceptive things to mankind that have likenesses to the plans and works of YHWH.

The story of Nimrod, Simeranus, and Tammuz who later became deified has transcended the Babylonian Empire and identifies your covenant with Satan today. In every kingdom, they have had names. They were Nimrod and Simiramis in Babylon, Isis and Osiris in Egypt, Ashtoreth and Baal in Phoenicia, Aphrodite and Adonis in Greece, and Venus and Cupid in Rome. The same statues that symbolize Nimrod and Simiramis have been renamed in each empire, and today their customs and statues have been married to the customs and statues of Christians so much that most people cannot identify Christian from pagan.

The symbol of Nimrod, Semiramis, and Tammuz was the sun, moon, and stars alongside human statues that bear their witness. These symbols have become the foundation of modern day paganism and the church.

Added onto the deified family of Nimrod have been many other pagan gods. Ischtar is another very common god that marks the marriage covenant of Satan in the lives of many people who call themselves Christian. She was a lover of Tammuz. She is said to be the "mother goddess", the goddess of fertility, generative powers, love and cruelty. Ischtar has been symbolized using the eight-pointed star and the planet Venus.

Since the Babylonian empire, she has been celebrated on the first Sunday after the vernal equinox. The Ischtar priest would impregnate young virgins on the altar and babies from the previous year would be sacrificed. The eggs of Ischtar would be dipped in the blood of the sacrificed babies which is the origin of dyed eggs in modern days with the customary color across the world being red (even at the US White House). The Ischtar service is the origin of the sun rise Sunday service at the vernal equinox we call Easter today. The name Ischtar is still used, but slightly modified. Hams are killed and eaten in honor of the sun god, Nimrod or the son of the sun god, Tammuz. In commemoration of the death and resurrection of the sun god. The 40 days of lent originated from the 40 years of the life of Tammuz commemorated by the 40 days of fasting and praying for Tammuz before Ischtar service.

Other gods have been added onto the foundation story of Nimrod, Semiramis, Tammuz, and Ischtar. The replicas of these people changes in name depending on setting, and today many people who call themselves Christian are adorning their homes with these statues. They buy the same replicas because they have become familiar with them as statues of Yeshua, Mary, and the disciples.

In your marriage covenant with Yeshua, he asked you not to make any images of any likeness; not even His own. Exodus 20:4-6 says:

You shall not make for yourself an idol, whether in the form of anything that is in heaven above, or is on the earth beneath, or that is in the water under the earth. You shall not bow down to them or worship them; for I the Lord your God am a jealous God, punishing children for the iniquity of parents, to the third and the fourth generation of those who reject me, but showing steadfast love to the thousandth generation of those who love me and keep my commandments.

Today, pagan symbols, the symbols I am certain bring tears to Yeshua' eyes; the symbols that have marked centuries of sacrificed babies, idol worship, and betrayal adorn the homes of many people who call themselves Christian. The mark of the beast within the homes is an open door for the entry of the enemy. Pine cones, pine trees, moons, stars, planets, tridents (pitchforks), statues of angels, people, crosses, and body parts adorn the homes of many people. Most people have attempted to re-associate the symbols with another cause, but what they mean to Yeshua and Satan is really what matters; not what they mean to you.

Statues containing the sun are one of the foundational symbols of paganism. Statues with the crescent moon holding the sun (Semiramis and her deceased husband) have been a symbol that commemorates Nimrod, Semiramis, and Tammuz for centuries. The Catholic Eucharist is a common way this symbolism of the sun inside of the crescent moon or simply the sun, moon, and stars are introduced as hidden symbols to many Christian households. The communion dishes many times are created in symbolism of the sun inside the crescent moon and we defile the act of transforming our DNA into Yeshua' when we engage in this act on a plate that symbolizes the martyrdom of many innocent people for Satan's pleasure.

The cross was originally a symbol of the sun and its rays. Sometimes the symbol would appear as a circle with eight rays extending from it, and sometimes, its symbol would be displayed as a cross. Many people wore necklaces of it to represent their allegiance to the sun god. When Yeshua came and died, he was not telling you to go, buy a cross and commemorate it. He was telling you, I am more powerful than the sun, the moon, and the stars. At his death, the entire Earth shook and the sun was blackened. He is not the sun god. He is the YHWH of the entire heavens (including the sun, moon, stars, galaxies, everything beyond the realms we see) and the Earth.

The trident is an ancient hand symbol appears like "devil's pitchfork" to represent the power of the gods of the sun. It has been placed on many historic statues, in a lot of ancient artwork, and on many monuments. Many cartoons, entertainers, and government officials hold the pitchfork symbol with their hands and the symbol has become a common icon. People who call themselves Christian may watch movies (such as Spiderman) and mimic him, and become accustomed to wielding this symbol.

The pagan statue of Jupiter with the halo represents the power of the sun god. The Vatican (the headquarters of the Roman Catholic Church) has a statue many people have become familiar with calling St. Peter with a sun crown on his head. Many people buy statues of Yeshua on the cross with a sun on his head thinking that the sun is the crown of thorns. The statue of liberty is also a representation of ancient pagan gods with the sun crowning his head. Rid your home of the graven images regardless of what you call them, they defile your temple.

The pine tree with its pine cones symbolized fertility goddesses. The pine tree stays green all year around so it is held as a pagan representation of constant fertility. This symbol is found on the staff of the catholic pope, and therefore has become a common icon in the homes of people who follow him and call themselves Christian. Our Christmas tree has also become a way that we commemorate the fertility goddess in our homes.

The sunburst or solar wheel or 8 pointed star or sun discs looks like a halo but represents pagan sun god worship. The star is the same star that is placed onto the Christmas tree; not the star of Bethlehem.

With the knowledge of the days, times, and the evil mixing of pagan and Christian, Charles Spurgeon said:

"We HAVE NO superstitious regard for times and seasons. Certainly we do not believe in the present ecclesiastical arrangement called Christmas: first, because we do not believe in the mass at all, but abhor it, whether it be said or sung in Latin or in English; and, secondly, because we find no Scriptural warrant whatever for observing any day as the birthday of the Saviour; and, consequently, its observance is a superstition, because not of divine authority."

Odin was a Scandinavian god of intoxicating drinks and ecstasy, as well as, the god of death. Odin was the god of wisdom, magic, occult knowledge, poetry, war, and death. The symbol of Odin (a big man with a white long beard) became Santa Claus. Santa Claus entering thru the chimney came from a Norse religion that the god would enter thru the chimney and bless the home.

The obelisk adorns the majority of today's churches marking the church's covenant with Satan. Obelisk means "Baal's shaft" or Baal's organ of reproduction. It is always placed in the center of a circle to represent the female genitalia and the sexual act. It stands as a tower with a pointed top. The Obelisk is located in the center of the Vatican, in Turkey, Cleopatra's needle, Scotland, Switzerland, in Germany, in France, Mecca, Egypt, Argentina, Amsterdam, Mongolia, Ethiopia, throughout the US (with the Washington monument being very popular), and is the origin of church steeples.

The things we do remind Him of the worship, the children sacrificed, the pouring out of blood as sacrifices to Satan. Google the terms I have used. Go thru your home and remove the altars of Baal and Ashtoreth! Burn them and rededicate your home to the marriage covenant of Yahshua!

The Mark of The Beast In Your Subjection To Pagan Calendars and Clocks

The wisdom of the times and seasons was given to Adam by YHWH. This knowledge was commemorated by his sons and written and expounded upon by Enoch. They understood the sun marked their appointments with their Dad, their Maker, and they recognized the position of the solar system with excitement. The Bible gives us wisdom on the times and seasons; this wisdom distinguishes the bride of Yahshua from the bride of Satan. With the investment of your time, you are making clear whose appointments and whose sacrifices you are willing to show up for and provide. The book of Enoch is very specific in how many days are in a year, how many months are in a year, and the celebrations YHWH desires to use to make His covenant with His bride. The sun, moon, and stars are supposed to be the signs we use to stay informed of when our date nights come with our Savior. The calendar and the clock has become a tool used to defile the times of YHWH and subject many people including those who call themselves Christian as slaves to time and pagan holy days.

Every pagan empire has attempted to change the calendar to re-align with their holy days and desecrate the sign of YHWH on His people. Babylon, Egypt, Persia, Greece, and Rome have all had modified calendars that recognized their pagan gods. Today, most people are speaking and subjecting themselves to the order of pagan gods by way of the modern-day calendar.

The modern day calendar began in 46 AD with Roman, Julius Caesar. His proposed calendar was 365.25 days long. The days of the week changed with the change of the calendar. The Romans named the days of the week after their gods and corresponded to the planets, the sun, and moon.

Sunday - Sun god

Monday - Moon god

Tuesday - associated with the planet Mars and the Norse god of war

Wednesday - Associated with the planet Mercury, god named Odin, associated with wisdom, magic, victory and death (his picture is modified to create the modern day Santa Claus)

Thursday - Associated with the planet Jupiter and the Norse god of thunder, strength and protection.

Friday is named after the wife of Odin. Some scholars say her name was Frigg; others say it was Freya; other scholars say Frigg and Freya were two separate goddesses. Associated with Venus, the Roman goddess of love, beauty and fertility.

As for Saturday - associated with the planet Saturn.

The calendar gained 3 days every four centuries, so the equinoxes and solstices were not properly aligned which threw off the accuracy of their pagan worship. Thus, the Julian calendar was modified with the Gregorian calendar in 1582 AD.

Pope Gregory proposed the Gregorian Calendar which became the official Roman calendar in 1582 AD. Most of the early church did not accept this calendar and actually fought against it. It made the year 365.2425 days long. The modification was requested by Pope Gregory because it changed the day of Easter so it fell closer to the vernal equinox for accuracy to Ischtar's worship.

The biblical calendar is 364 days long with YHWH's appointed days throughout and Jubilees. This was given before the law. The Books of Enoch, Jasher, Jubilees, Adam and Eve 1 and 2 in addition to other commentaries will confirm the feast days were given to Adam as appointed dates of communion between Father and son. The days of the week are counted as first day, second day, third day, until the Sabbath. The months were counted by YHWH as first month (where the first day is marked by equal day and night), second month, and so on. The Hebrew names of the months originated mostly from the literal translation of "first month, second month" an association with a harvested crop, or a correlation with the constellation seen overhead in the Hebrew language. The calendar is also specifically aligned so that adherents can be recipients of the supernaturally opened gates of specific times of the year. Gates are used for blessing and judgment. They release rain, frost, thunder, lightning, winds, and much more.

The Bible provides promises to those who wear the mark of His marriage covenant, and if the gates are tampered with by the enemy, you can override his illegal authority when you are aware of the times of YHWH. These names are currently recognized on the closest biblically-maintained calendar: the Jewish calendar. Rather than the constant assumption thru the pagan time-keeping that one hour is 60 minutes, an hour is defined as 1/12 of the time from sunrise to sunset. During the winter, an hour can be much less than 60 minutes, and during the summer, it can be more than 60 minutes.

The enemy currently tampers a lot with the gates controlling the weather, but most people are subjected to pagan calendars and pagan systems of thought rendering them powerless in regard to weather regulation for the Kingdom. When the enemy operates a gate at a time not appointed or when the gates of judgment are opened and you have been walking in the frequency of righteousness, you can close them. When a gate of blessing can be opened or you can be a recipient thru a gate of blessing, you can exercise your authority to receive, but only when you are aware. YHWH told David:

Therefore the wicked will not stand in the judgment,

nor sinners in the congregation of the righteous;

for the Lord watches over the way of the righteous,

but the way of the wicked will perish. (Psalms 1:5-6)

And later, He told Solomon:

Righteousness guards one whose way is upright, but sin overthrows the wicked. (Proverbs 13:6)

Therefore, if the enemy attempts to manipulate the weather around you, and you wear the mark of the covenant of Yahshua, you should not be shaken, and you will prevail in overthrowing his plans. If a frost comes and the Bible says the chamber of the frost is not supposed to be open at that time, you can rebut it, but if you are not aware or not walking upright, you cannot. Remember, He said, His sheep hear His voice and His voice speaks thru nature, but if you are unaware, you will not hear His voice. Learn the times and seasons of YHWH, align with them, and govern in your right power.

The days Yeshua told us are special to him, our special date nights with him are the feast days. In the time of the Roman Empire, the pagan holidays were merged with Christian customs. December 25th was the birth date of Nimrod and Tammuz, we have called it Christmas and said Yeshua was born that day. Yeshua' birth date was not discussed in the Bible. Because of the records of the stars, many have correlated an astronomical one-time event occurring on the feast of tabernacles (held in September) in the year of Yeshua' birth, and presumed He could have been born then. Regardless, the Bible does not tell us Yeshua' birth should be celebrated, and it especially says nothing about December 25th.

Ischtar was the date of child sacrifice. We have called it Easter and commemorated it with eggs, bunnies, and ham.

Tammuz was incestuous with his mother. He is commemorated as a baby with a bow and arrow called Cupid. A holiday has been created to celebrate his incestuous affair and we call it Valentine's day.

Early Christians worshipped on Saturday, Shabbat, the Sabbath. The change of the day of worship took place between 363 and 365 AD during the seven ecumenical councils of Laodicea. The calendar was changed to suit sun god worshippers' interest labeling every day of the week after a deity they worshipped. The charge deity being the sun god commemorated on "Sun-day". The covenant that marks the worship and marriage date night with Satan is commemorated weekly by people who call themselves Christian thru Sunday morning "Sun rise" services.

Satan is not selective about names. He does not care if you go and say you are showing allegiance to YHWH on Sunday. He is only concerned with bending the ways and requests YHWH has ordained in His marriage covenant with you. Many have said, "Yeshua rose on Sunday, so I worship on Sunday because of his resurrection". Did He ask you to do that? Some say, "I celebrate Yeshua' birth on Christmas". Did He ask you to do that? Do what He asked you to do!

If my husband asked me to do something and another man

comes and asks me to do something even if it's slightly different, he is angered by it. He is made in the image of YHWH and every married man whose wife honors another man's words over his will tell you they are angered anytime that happens. Satan is the other guy. He doesn't really care if he doesn't have your full attention because as long as he is the "side" guy, he knows that eventually (at death), he will have you. Be vigilant!

Regarding the mark of the beast, Revelations 20:4 says:

Then I saw thrones, and those seated on them were given authority to judge. I also saw the souls of those who had been beheaded for their testimony to Yeshua and for the word of YHWH. They had not worshiped the beast or its image and had not received its mark on their foreheads or their hands. They came to life and reigned with Yahshua a thousand years.

Using the law of first mention, the first time a mark was placed on the forehead and on the hand, YHWH was referring to His appointed times. The appointed times are a distinguishing mark between Yeshua and His bride. For this reason, He said:

"Seven days you shall eat unleavened bread, and on the seventh day there shall be a festival to the Lord. Unleavened bread shall be eaten for seven days; no leavened bread shall be seen in your possession, and no leaven shall be seen among you in all your territory. You shall tell your child on that day, 'It is because of what the Lord did for me when I came out of Egypt.' It shall serve for you as a sign on your hand (your tool for implementation) and as a reminder on your forehead (your house of decision-making), so the teaching of the Lord may be on your lips; for with a strong hand the Lord brought you out of Egypt. You shall keep this ordinance at its proper time from year to year."

With the scripture in mind, you can choose whose mark you will wear. For me, I will be wearing the mark of Yeshua!

The Mark of The Beast In Your Allegiance To The Education Process

Most people are unaware of the revelation I am giving because of the process of education. Christians have surrendered their ammunition to the authority of a pagan education system. Wisdom is ammunition that is given from Heaven to people on Earth. No degree or credentials identify a person's training with the spirit of wisdom. Righteousness identifies a person whose inherited wisdom. Children are not learning how to be priests and ambassadors, parents have relied on their education for success, and generations of people have been taught to surrender their currency to an institutionalized system; dissolving the power of the majority of the people who call themselves Christian.

School systems fill the student's time with the basic tenets to uphold their plans of a one world order. When Yeshua sends provisions, most people are at a loss of how to convert it into the currency of their time. People disbelieve and disapprove of YHWH's messengers on the basis of whether or not they have a degree or pagan assigned credential. They do not listen unless the person has submitted themselves to the subjective process that usually causes many to become enslaved by debt, false teaching, and slave mentalities in pagan school systems.

The current education system governing the Western world originated in the Babylonian Empire at the time of Noah. A common language, system of numbers, system of writing, customs, and courtesies were taught to advance the pagan cause of Nimrod. Their goal was to unite the people to build a tower and overthrow YHWH.

Today a common language, system of thought, system of entertainment (Hollywood, Cartoon Network, etc.), standard of success, and standard of education has indoctrinated most people to the point they are deaf to the voice and see the ways YHWH desires for them to live. This is a sign of the covenant of the devil incepted in the Babylonian Empire that ended in judgment and the confusion of languages at the tower of Babel.

You MUST return to your first love! Return to hearing and seeing what He is saying. You cannot sift what He is saying thru your Babylonian, Egyptian, Greek, Persian, or Roman indoctrination called "a school education". Remove that mark of the beast from your ways!

The Mark Of The Beast In Your Character

How you act towards friends, how you act towards family, how you act towards strangers, and how you act towards your enemies, does it reflect your covenant with Yeshua, or does it identify you with Satan? It's not only about the image you put on in public. Yeshua visits you in public and in private. The Holy Spirit is omnipresent. He is with you at the grocery store, in your kitchen, in your shower, and as you sit on the toilet. Angels and demons are reporting your workings done publicly and privately.

Sometimes, when you have chosen to just "chill", your throwing clothes around, being disorganized, and giving the excuse, "I'll come back to it later". What covenant do you exemplify in your level of organization? What covenant do you exemplify in your "chill" mentality? Does it identify you with Yeshua or with Satan? When you hear a new challenge or a call to draw closer to YHWH (such as this), what covenant do you exemplify? Doubt? Isolation? Frustration? In your most frustrating moments, are you reflecting the mark of Yeshua: love, joy, peace, patience, gentleness, kindness, and self-control? Or, are you reflecting drunkenness, sorcery (drug-use included), witchcraft, immorality, idolatry, factions, debauchery, discord, hatred, fits of rage, and the marks that identify you with the flesh or with the enemy? When your child misbehaves, what covenant does your parenting exemplify? When your spouse disagrees with you or does not support you, what covenant do you exemplify? In your most trying times, what covenant do you exemplify? Character building is like chiseling dense stone. It requires work, intention, pruning, pain, discipline, and persistence. Your character should reflect the virtues of the covenant with Yeshua. Remove the mark from your character, change your habits, and align with the covenant of YHWH.

The Mark Of The Beast Seen In Your Health Care Plans

Diabetes, heart failure, cancer, blood disease, blood pressure problems, and many other health ailments are common in our world today. They are there because a door has been open to the kingdom in darkness that has not been closed. They have been able to uphold a birth defect. They have been able to maintain the confines of a curse. They have been able to enter into the presence of YHWH when you are not there, or they have been able to tempt you enough you bowed, and they entered; marking you in your health. Most people run to a pagan medical care system as a first resort to restore their health. Isn't that an oxymoron? Satan stamps you with his mark, then you go and ingrain it deeper by asking him for healing. The Bible never grants authority to anyone to exercise health relief to His bride accept His priests. Your marriage contract with Him says you place no other gods before him: not medicine, not healthcare, not doctors.

Today, the majority of the natural resources, agriculture, and even the water supplies are subjected to the tampering of the kingdom of darkness. In Leviticus 19:19, YHWH said:

"You shall keep my statutes. You shall not let your animals breed with a different kind; you shall not sow your field with two kinds of seed; nor shall you put on a garment made of two different materials."

Yet, fallen angels have infiltrated many minds with the idea of genetically modifying seeds, mixing animals of different kinds, gender adjustments, and tampering with DNA of every sort. The seeds and fruits of evil are being sold and distributed everywhere and may be as close as your own refrigerator. The modified foods are the cheapest and a sacrifice to YHWH is required for each decision you make to honor Him even when there is a significant price difference.

You do not want the mark of the beast identifying you by the way you eat, the markings on your body, the way you dress, or your resort when you have an ailment. The mark identifies the recipients of the beast's judgment. If you do not want the judgment, remove the mark, and renew your covenant to YHWH! Place the mark of the covenant of YHWH by listening to His words to you, His bride, honoring His words, and applying them to your life without regard of the cost.

Chemicals can be found in just about anything. The enemy has provided several tactics to mankind to control you in the area of health. Your temple is sacred and sorcery defiles it. The Bible defines sorcery as the use of things other than instructed by YHWH to manipulate the ways of the world to include your body.

YHWH can instruct you to visit a doctor or to use a medication, but you must submit the determination to Him and wait for an answer. The mark of the beast in your healthcare plan is in how you maintain your body. When an ailment occurs and your first response is to react aside from seeking YHWH, this confirms your ways are not subjected to YHWH. You are not a living sacrifice. You wear the identity and walk in the ways of the beast. When you go to the grocery store, and you ask, "What do I want?", "What do I have a taste for?", or you found your decisions on humane desires, you are not a living sacrifice. You should be saying, "You said you wanted me to have life, therefore, I need to purchase things that align with your will, and not mine." Mute the flesh and make choices from the spirit. Yeshua would look in many people's grocery cart and see the mark of the beast, the fruits of the flesh, and no sign of a covenant with Him. Is that you? He would look at the dress of many people and recall the same attire on those who have sacrificed his innocent babies, who do witchcraft, and who spit in his face. Who do you want to remind Him of?

Your eating, your body adornments, dress, lotions, perfumes, and everything else you use to care for your temple should be subjected to the authority of Yeshua. Ask Him, "Does this identify my covenant with Yeshua or does this identify me with Satan?" Act on what He says.

The Mark of The Beast In The Company You Keep

You are responsible for choosing good company. Your company associates you with the covenant of YHWH or the covenant of the enemy. Every interaction must be preceded the one cause: advancing the Kingdom of Heaven. You cannot keep comfort food as friends; people who tell you things to make you feel better. No! You are a living sacrifice. You choose your company from His criteria; not yours. You need to keep people around you who stimulate your cause: advancing the Kingdom of Heaven. You cannot entertain people who obviously have no intentions to walk upright! They are yeast. Paul said, "A little bit of yeast ruins the whole batch". Do not be that batch.

The Mark Of The Beast In Your Entertainment

What do you do in your "down time"? What do you do when you're off work and you choose how to spend your time? Music, televisions shows, concerts, plays, and entertainers all can make the choice to be in covenant with Yeshua or Satan. Your connection with them by way of investing your time in taking in their fruit, places the mark of their allegiance on you. Does their music connect you with those who please YHWH or does it identify you with those who do not? Every second of the day should be dedicated to a unified cause: advancing the Kingdom of Heaven on Earth. If you think, "This looks like a good show" or "I like the beat in this song", but it has no connection to advancing the Kingdom of Heaven, you are not a living sacrifice. It is black and white. Either you are multiplying what YHWH is giving you (including your time and your example) exemplifying your covenant with YHWH or Satan. It's simple. Look at what you're watching, you're listening to, and everything else that is entering your gates. Analyze the reason you have subjected yourself to its influence. Remove the mark of the beast and place Yeshua as a seal on your heart.

The Mark Of The Beast In Subjecting Your Money To Pagan Authorities

Today, the responsibilities of the priests have been surrendered to the government and other pagan run industries; placing them as authoritarian between the marriage covenant of most believers and YHWH. They must take currency from a secular institution and give it to the church rather than receiving from YHWH and using currency to administer the Kingdom citizens to Him.

Yeshua said, "Give what is Caesar's to Caesar", so I am not saying you should not pay your taxes! However, there should be supremacy in your YHWH-given currency (intellectual property, wisdom, ideas, connections, etc.), and you should not subject that to pagan authorities.

Many churches have subjected their ministries to pagan authorities signing 501C3 and other documents vowing the entity will not profit. How can the Kingdom be expanded without currency and profit? Where in the Bible do you find a church that did not operate in the role of the bank? As a result, they heighten wages, do campaigns that YHWH has not directed them to do, and manipulate their inheritance to align with the will of the pagan authorities that their ministry does not profit. Churches subject everything they bring in their storehouses to the awareness and manipulation of pagan authorities, and people connected have become subjected simply by way of attachment.

Just as all men of YHWH feel the responsibility of caring for their brides, Yeshua provides for his bride. The problem is that most people are looking for the currency of another to provide and sustain them. Yeshua does not send dollars, Euros, Cedis, or any other type of man-made currency from Heaven. He does not maintain world-made interests in His treasuries. Contrarily, He provides the things that precede man's adaptation: ideas, solutions, connections, faith, cures, strength, opportunities, etc. At times, He will even leave gold dust, gems, or bars that supercede the Earth's in quality. He leaves things that cannot be calculated on Earth's value scales.

You must divorce the devil. Do not be dependent on his supply for you, but rather revert to Yeshua' ways. He is the High priest. You present yourself as a living sacrifice to Him, and go to Him when you have ANY needs, and He will provide for you.

In the Old Testament, YHWH spoke to Moses requiring each family deposit money into the treasury of the Levite priests. Taxes and banking were governed by the Levitical priesthood thru tithes, sacrifices, and offerings. These enabled the priest to expand the domain of the Kingdom of Heaven on Earth. If a person had any divine concern to include health, funding, relationships, justice, or anything else, the priest was to administer the mandate of Heaven for that person. Most people have surrendered this same ethic to the expansion of the kingdom of darkness thru the same system with pagan motives.

Governments and banking systems are using the funding system that has been altered and manipulated from its biblical inception, and used it to expand the kingdom of darkness. People who call themselves Christian have a difficult time implementing tithing, offering, and New Testament sacrifice principles because they do not understand if they do not increase the treasuries of the administration of the Kingdom of Heaven on Earth, then the kingdom in darkness will reign over them in government, justice, media, entertainment, health. When this happens, they will not be able to find a way out because they have fallen victim to their own choices.

I am not telling you to start giving to a church without discernment. Most churches are guilty of making the same covenant with Satan that you have. Make a choice. Either become a vessel for administering the Kingdom of Heaven priesthood and use the tithes, offerings, and sacrifices to ensure this is fulfilled, or, find a church (however small or large) that does not have connections with the satanic covenant, and is actively administering and expanding the Kingdom of Heaven on Earth, release the biblically recommended tithes, offerings, and New Testament sacrifices to them! Do not look for the title "church" or the building of a church, but rather look for the function of the priest being fulfilled thru a human entity, and sow.

Joseph Lumpkin said, "Rome made church an institution. America made church a business". We are supposed to expand out, not up. You are not looking for a huge hierarchy, you are looking for the fruits of executed expansion: people being taught truth, people becoming spiritually mature, people being healed and delivered, people being directed for entrance into Heaven; this is church. It can be one person fulfilling the mandate that is a church. It can be you. I am a church. You are a church.

Using the law of first mention, the concept of banking originated in the Bible where it speaks of YHWH placing Adam in charge of His wealth on the Earth (Genesis 3). Adam was the first banker and his responsibility was to multiply what he had been given. Adam spoke to someone other than YHWH who manipulated the agreement by making him feel like he deserved more from the transaction. The serpent told him he could be like YHWH, rather than simply in charge of His treasury and government administration. Adam forsook the agreement he had with YHWH, and placed Satan in authority of all of YHWH's wealth that was placed in his care.

You make the same choice every time YHWH pours ideas, connections, opportunities, talents, and solutions to you, and rather than multiplying them for the advancement of the Kingdom, you focus yourself on the enemy's strategy for financial gain. Some people have postponed ideas because they are occupying their time with alternative work for money. Just as YHWH placed Adam in charge of the whole world, he has also given you territories, and you are His banker. You can choose to yield everything that He gives you to the care of Satan, and as an adulterous woman, you can expect to infuriate your eternal Husband and Saviour.

Abel was blessed when he presented a multiplied and quality return back to YHWH, whereas Cain was not because he had kept the best portion for himself and given the remainder to YHWH.

Many large corporations have infuriated their clients for the same reason that YHWH was infuriated with Cain. Corporations like Enron, who have clients that invest millions of dollars expecting to receive high returns on their investments when contrarily, the leaders take the largest portion of the return and give low returns (or possibly no returns) to their clients. Most Enron clients did not even receive all of their original investment back. The clients were enraged for the same reason YHWH was enraged with Cain.

If YHWH has instructed you to do something, push back against your wallet! Push back against your debit card balance! Push back against your bread and water! Know that He will provide for you, so look for the materialization. Do not let doubt push you around!

You are a priest in the order of Melchizedek

Hebrews 7:1-3 says:

This "King Melchizedek of Salem, priest of the Most High God, met Abraham as he was returning from defeating the kings and blessed him"; and to him Abraham apportioned "one-tenth of everything." His name, in the first place, means "king of righteousness"; next he is also king of Salem, that is, "king of peace." Without father, without mother, without genealogy, having neither beginning of days nor end of life, but resembling the Son of YHWH, he remains a priest forever.

He was the first priest written of in the Bible. Aaron was used to exemplify a comparison role for the people of the Earth. The priest was held responsible for:

- The treasury of Israel
- The sacrifices of Israel
- He was in charge of the most valuable things in Israel
- He was in charge of health maintenance
- He was in charge of speaking to YHWH
- He was in charge of the cleanliness of the land
- He was in charge of teaching the ways of the Lord
- He was in charge of maintaining an atmosphere of worship (musicians, intercessors, prophets)
- He was in charge of the administration of the Kingdom of Heaven on the Earth
- He was in charge of maintaining the temple and all of its sacred things
- He was in charge of the justice system
- He was in charge of disseminating messages and order
- He was in charge of training other priests assigned to the people of Israel

Melchizedek is the first priest mentioned in the Bible. He is mentioned as a priest of the Most High. He is not a priest of an

Earthly temple, but rather a priest of Heaven. Yeshua is the High priest. The responsibilities Aaron had on Earth are the responsibilities Melchizedek administers in Heaven. He has a larger realm of authority and impact because Heaven is the origin of all of the Earth's workings. Yeshua is the King of Kings even in charge of Melchezedik. Yeshua governs Heaven righteously and is the head in charge of all of YHWH's creation and more. Melchizedek governs the priestly portion of Heaven's affairs.

The marriage contract that you have with Yeshua tells you that when He gives you currency, you are to: (1) Put 10% aside for the advancement of His Kingdom on Earth (as is performed by the priest - you), (2) Invest in making arrangements nice for visitors/foreigners (3) Set aside provisions for the widows, orphans, and the poor (4) Set aside some for date nights (otherwise called Sabbath, firstfruit offerings given the 1st of each month, feast days) and gifts, and when this is complete, He will ensure what you have left is more than enough for your needs to be met. When you do not fulfill ANY of the above things that Yeshua has instructed you to do with what He gives you, He knows you are placing an idol between you and your covenant with Him; breaking the first covenant promise He gave you. Debt is not the fault of YHWH, but it is your personal choice to be tied to an entity so that you can have whatever you traded for. Debt or anything else should not come before YHWH.

The Bible tells us that as priests we are to bring sacrifices with love before YHWH. Many people have brought sacrifices with lust to their flesh and accordingly, have been bound in debt. When you look at your bank statement, are you greatest sacrifices for your debt, your car, your house, birthdays, for Christmas, or for the things and days that YHWH has asked for? If so, analyze your heart of love towards YHWH. Who do you love most: creation or the Creator? Do not be like Cain (Adam's son who did not please YHWH with his sacrifice). Do the most to advance the Kingdom on the days that YHWH recommended. Spend the most money on the things that YHWH instructed you to. Do the most to serve others on the days that YHWH recommended. Give the most on the days that YHWH recommended and tear down the altars where you have sacrificed to the enemy (Halloween, Christmas, flesh-worship birthday parties, etc.). Keep the focus on staying close to your first love, being a living sacrifice, and serving Him. The first covenant promise says, "You shall have no other gods before me". Bad stewardship is breaking the marriage covenant with Yeshua and entertaining a mistress.

Being in the order of Melchizedek means you have been placed in charge of a portion of the treasury of Heaven. Banks do not have more authority of currency than you. They may have more authority of their specific printed currency, but more valuable forms of currency have only been authorized for regulation from YHWH to His priest and bride. Satan was thrown out of Heaven for ungodly trading, and if he were to attempt to step between the authority given to you by YHWH, He would be thrown out again (unless you authorized it). The responsibilities given to Melchizedek in Heaven are the responsibilities given to you on Earth. For this reason, Hebrews 5:19-20 says:

We have this hope, a sure and steadfast anchor of the soul, a hope that enters the inner shrine behind the curtain, where Yeshua, a forerunner on our behalf, has entered, having become a high priest forever according to the order of Melchizedek.

We are priests administering the Kingdom of YHWH on the Earth with the responsibilities that Aaron had in Israel and Melchizedek has in Heaven. What you are given, you are supposed to multiply for the advancement of the Kingdom. When the King gives you an idea, He wants to see many people impacted for the Kingdom with that idea because He has placed you in charge of it. He has given you the portion that you have so that you can use it to fulfill your governmental role and colonize the Earth. Stay away from the trading floors of the enemy by placing your talents, your ideas, your time, or anything else YHWH has given you into subjection to secular sources.

We must remove jobs, banks, and others as intermediaries between the flow of currency between Heaven and the royal priesthood. Jobs can be good when they position you where you can use the currency YHWH has given you for the advancement of His Kingdom. They become bad when you are subjected to it, abandoning that YHWH has given you to trade for money (a currency within Satan's realm of authority). When YHWH adds more to your treasury of authority, you MUST seek Him about how to multiply it rather than storing it under the soil of excuses or dependency.

The mark of the beast is similar to a wedding ring. It is a visible way that you can be identified as dominion of Satan. Many say it will be a chip under the skin or a barcode on the forehead; this I do not know, but I do know that the mark can be seen in your ways. Remove the mark and wear the sign of His covenant: the times and seasons (Gen 1:14), obedience to multiply and advance His Kingdom, and obedience to the laws.

Exercise

Now we have discussed how the mark of the beast can be seen in your ways. We need to clear that out and restore the mark of Yeshua.

1. Go thru your house, look for things that identify you with fruitless ways. Look for things that distract or deter you away from Yeshua. Look for things you have an addictive relationship with. This can include anything: blankets, books, television, tablets, and computers. We are not talking about mission-essential business or school items. We are looking for things you have an unhealthy addiction to: food, garments, etc. Things that cause the mark of the beast to be displayed in your character need to be removed. These things are idols. Remove them.
2. Go thru your house and look for things with the symbols that we discussed: the cross, the sun, statues, pine cones, pine trees, and any other graven images. I found the symbols on books, on Christian scripture hangings, on decorative items, on cartoon images, and on clothing. Look carefully.
3. Log onto your bank accounts or look at the records for your currency (your schedule, checkbook, web banking, talents, ideas, etc.). Who gets the most of your currency: leisure, your flesh, your debt, or the Kingdom? Do you give more money for birthdays than you do for feasts? Do you invest more time on Thanksgiving than you do for Sabbaths? Do you think more about money than you do developing your relationship with Yeshua? The first commandment tells us not to have any other gods before Him,

and our gods can many times be seen on our bank statements. You can see who gets the majority of your sacrifices of time, money, gifts, and others. If you have noticed the mark of the beast in your currency, repent, and create a strategy to abandon the present ideology. If you spend the majority of your money on debt, make a plan to remove the debt, make more money, and advance the Kingdom with your currency. If you spend more time on secular activities, make a plan to seek after righteousness in your unique way. Seek YHWH then carry out His orders.

4. Rededicate your health plan to YHWH. Make a vow. Analyze your refrigerator. Are the things in there to appease your taste buds, or do they supply your body with the necessities for long life? Get rid of things that feed your flesh! This may include sweets, ice cream, and junk food. This includes anything that threatens your life.

   For my family, we live on mostly vegetables and fruits, less than 50% meat in each meal, reverse osmosis treated water, rice, wheat, beans, and the like. Sweets are very closely guarded and a very low inventory stays in the house. It was a change for us and we did it. You can too.

   The change has to be done. People are dying everyday because they eat to please their flesh. Eating to feed the flesh (whether it's digested or entertained) is the #1 killer internationally. It causes slow unhealthy death or quick homicidal deaths. Do not feed your flesh. Throw everything away that does that! Mute the voices in your mind that tell you to do otherwise. Just do it!

Say, "YHWH. I declare this day that I will seek you first before I place anything in my shopping cart, before I turn my television or computer on, before I go to my medicine cabinet, or call for a doctor's appointment, I will seek you first, and I will wait patiently on your answer. I desire your mark to be placed over my life and your DNA to run thru my veins, so as I take this vow, I align my actions with your covenant, and I announce to Satan your time to leave is now! Pack your bags and go! The covenants you created with me or prior generations are canceled and paid for with the blood. I stand before the courts of YHWH, I plead guilty for the error of my ways, and I place the blood on (list your sins, health ailments, your home, and your family concerns). Father, the mark of your son distinguishes me in Yeshua' name I walk in freedom. Amen."

5. List your friends, go to your social media accounts, and see what marks identify them. Analyze whether your connection with them is consistent with your mandate from Yeshua and remove yeast.
6. List your daily activities. Is your time spent to feed your flesh, to feed the devil, or to grow your relationship with YHWH? Why do you do what you do with your time? If you have any cyclical things that you do with your time, write them down, and ask YHWH, "Is there any way I can take this time and make it more pleasing to you?" Place the mark of Yeshua on your time and your reason.
7. Go to your movie cabinet, your music, your game boards, your video games, and all of your other means of entertainment. Ask YHWH, "Is your mark on all of these things?" If you identify a mark of the beast on any of the things, throw them away. Don't put them in the indoor trash can; take them outside.

8. Sit down. List the frequent thoughts, ideas, talents, connections, words of prophesy, prayers, money, and all of your other means of currency. Ask YHWH and yourself, "Can I use these things to more effectively advance the Kingdom? How can I make these things a sweeter aroma to YHWH?"
9. Rededicate your temple (your home, your body, your family, etc.). This process is especially nice with communion and by using anointing oil. Pray over your thoughts, your actions, your stewardship, your connections and your property. Anoint them and dedicate them all to YHWH.

CHAPTER FOUR

KNOW YOUR BENEFITS

David and Shalom were a newlywed couple. Just two hours before, they said, "I do", and they were ecstatic to begin their life together. Their limousine took them to the airport, where they were traveling to the honeymoon they had planned for three months; a seven day trip to Bora Bora.

When they arrived to their hotel in Bora Bora, they gazed in one another's eyes, got lost in their caress, and soon felt hungry. They decided to walk one block away to a local restaurant to try the cuisine. While they were there, an odd exchange happened, but they did not pay it much attention. The waiter, began screaming saying, "I stepped on a nail or a piece of glass", and a fellow patron picked up their food and brought it to their table. Without concern or question, David and Shalom ate vigorously.

When they got back to their room, David began feeling sick. His temperature had spiked and he was sweating. Within two hours, his eyesight was completely altered. Shalom was asking, "Are you okay?", and David was unable to respond. Without much knowledge of how to handle his sickness overseas, Shalom began to panic. She ran out to the hotel front desk, and asked, "How do you call the paramedics?! My husband is sick!" The hotel manager said, "Don't worry. I will call and have them come to your room."

One half-hour later, the paramedics arrived to see David completely unconscious. They wheeled him away, and Shalom sobbed unendingly. She did not know what to do. Her mind kept pondering, "How are we going to pay for doctor's visit and doctor's stay in another country? Will our insurance cover the expenses here?" At the hospital, Shalom was told her husband would require surgery in order to live. They said, "Your husband has been poisoned. Please let us know if your insurance will cover the procedure, or if we should postpone the service; possibly risking his life." Shalom said, "Let me call my insurance company. When she called, the customer service specialist told her, "I'm sorry, but we do not cover health care received out of the country of residence". Shalom burst out in tears. "This cannot be happening!" she cried.

She went and sat alongside her husband at his bedside. Two hours later, his heart monitor began flat lining. "B-E-E-E-E-P-P-P!" is all that she heard in the hospital room, then the nurses and doctors ran in. Twenty minutes later, in the lobby a nurse walked out and said, "I'm sorry Mrs. Anderson. Your husband just passed away." Shalom sobbed. "This was supposed to be our honeymoon and instead, it's the worse day of my life!"

When she arrived back home to Michigan, Shalom decided to cancel her insurance and find another plan. When she called, the attendant said, "May I ask why you would like to cancel your insurance plan? This one is the highest rated plan in the country." Shalom responded, "I tried calling to get coverage on my vacation, and I was told I could not receive coverage in another country". "That is not true," the attendant said. "That is what I was told when my husband was on his death bed" said Shalom. "Where were you located?" the attendant asked. "We were in Bora Bora on our honeymoon" Shalom said. "My family is from Bora Bora and our family doctor lives there. We go home for all of our medical care and receive coverage from the same insurance plan your currently on". "My husband just passed away because of misinformation?" "I apologize ma'am. Do you know who you spoke with?" the attendant asked. "No" said Shalom. "I'm so sorry. We always tell our clients to read over their benefits, so that no one can misinform you".

You Were Sent As A Solution To World Turmoil

Every day, diseases are contracted, people are dying, relationships are dissolving, and someone misses a meal. YHWH is not happy with His creation suffering. He has provided the Way, the Truth, and Life for us all, but many are unaware of their benefits thru Yahshua!

Your Role As An Ambassador

2 Corinthians 5:20 says you are an ambassador of Yahshua. An ambassador deploys in representation of their country of nativity. You are a native to the Kingdom of Heaven if you have crowned Yeshua as Lord of your life. When He is your King, He entrusts you as a gate or access way to the goods of the Kingdom. Your assignment is to introduce the Earth's Kings to the added benefits they can receive by submitting their governess to the laws and rule of the Kingdom of Heaven.

Our roles can better be understood if we understand the role and duties of ambassadors serving in different areas of the national policy today. When deployed, a country's ambassador makes authoritative actions in representation of their native country. He represents, speaks and advocates for the country and its interest. His economy, though living in another nation is the same as that of his home country, and as though he is living at home.

His salary is not determined by the government of the nation where he is serving but by the sending nation. Even the embassies in those nations completely differ from everything in the host country. The ambassador has access to the treasury of their native country, and can transform the status of the host country for good or bad.

The ambassador's voice is like the voice of the president or king. He talks, and advocates for his country, he introduces the government and citizens of its host country to the policies and benefits of the sending country. A country that touches the Ambassador touches the country as a nation and its leader.

The World's Governments Are Facing Tragedies

Although the world's governments have come leaps and bounds with technology and the implementation of ideas, some problems will not have a tangible solution without importing goods from Heaven. While Earth's governments each offer some way to maintain health, no government can offer anything beyond treatments that are mixed together from Heaven's imported ingredients: water, plants, and ideas. Additionally, no company can ensure the same ratios of satisfaction as the Kingdom of Heaven.

Their healthcare policies do not work for 100% of the populace (if anyone); that is why you are different. The Kingdom you represent has health care that works for every one that believes. For He Himself took our infirmities and bore our sicknesses (Matthew 8:16-17). You were sent to announce the good news of YHWH's healthcare policy; how His eternal plan offers everyone complete healing. When Yeshua died on the cross, He paid duly for every curse, birth defect, sickness and disease that has ever come on man, and upon that basis, every disease is declared cured and every sickness declared healed by YHWH. For by the wounds of Yahshua, we are cured. (1 Peter 2:24). This is YHWH's health care program and it is good for all who hears and believes. Go tell this.

Their welfare policies do not work for 100% of the populace (if anyone). No nation on earth has been able to completely eradicate poverty from among its people; no government systems have been able to equitably and evenly distribute its resources; even in the wealthiest countries, there are still poor people. Deuteronomy 15:11 says, "There will always be poor people in the land. Therefore I command you to be open-handed toward your fellow Israelites who are poor and needy in your land." On recurring instances when Earth's Kings have submitted their governance to YHWH, He has taken them from poor to rich. For example in Genesis, YHWH gave Joseph the vision and the interpretation to the dream of the Pharoah of his land. When he relayed the dream and the interpretation to the Pharoah, he went from being a jail inmate to an advisor of the Egyptian Kingdom. Esther went from being a modest young orphan girl to the Queen of the richest kingdom of her time. David went from being a shepherd to being one of the most well-known Kings of Israel without family lineage or any added advantage except for YHWH's favor. Whether you govern a bedroom, a home, a family, a city, a state, a province, or a nation, when you submit your governance to YHWH, your relationship with YHWH, your access to walk alongside Yeshua thru the courts, mountains, gardens, and valleys of the Kingdom of YHWH will transform your life!

The Kingdom of Heaven is the Solution

YHWH's Kingdom is not like man's kingdom. YHWH's Son was made poor so that we through His poverty might be made rich; for as many who believe. Our Kingdom's welfare policy works 100 percent and works all the time for all people. Rather than money, revelation is deposited into the account of your heart and mind. You may hear the auditory voice of YHWH, you may see images you do not understand nor can you manipulate in the display of your imagination, you may see dreams, be paralyzed by a trance, YHWH may send someone to impart revelation into you; be attentive to the varying ways He speaks. Revelation is what elevates Kingdom citizens to their proper positions. Here are a few things YHWH reveals that will transform your life:

- Your Assignment

- Sources of favor

- Destiny-Helpers or paramount connection

- Areas of His Kingdom where your provisions are ripe to materialize on the Earth

- Ideas or witty inventions

- Himself - The Source of wisdom, prudence, discipline, assignment, creation.

- Your gifts - talents, passions, areas of increased wisdom, your story, or other unique details about yourself

- Equity in your property (For example: You could find gold in your possession today!)

Those who abide by Heaven's laws assuredly receive prosperity in health, wealth, and relationships.

Earth's taxation systems are not always fair; some show partiality to rich, and some show partiality to the poor. I have never seen any nation where there are no tax evaders and offenders. Even the strictest of government every year takes people to court who are liable in the area of taxation and still some individuals get away with it. But YHWH's kingdom is not so.

The Bible clearly says that neither rich nor poor should receive partiality. Leviticus 19:15 says, "'Do not pervert justice; do not show partiality to the poor or favoritism to the great, but judge your neighbor fairly." In Heaven's taxes are measurements of obedience rather than a supplier for the economy. When obedience is recognized, increase is returned. Malachi 3:10-12 says, "Bring the whole tithe into the storehouse, there may be food in my house. Test me in this," says the Lord Almighty, "and see if I will not throw open the floodgates of heaven and pour out so much blessing there will not be room enough to store it. I will prevent pests from devouring your crops, and the vines in your fields will not drop their fruit before it is ripe," says the Lord Almighty. "Then all the nations will call you blessed, for yours will be a delightful land," says the Lord Almighty." All other tax systems tax citizens for supply to the economy, and do not have the ability to grant increase. No economy and tax system can be fairer than Heaven's.

Your Benefits

The earth is copying heaven; the real is there, while we do a photocopy is down this way. Everything that earth tries to do is a mimic on the things that are in heaven. Yet even at that, the earth is lagging behind.

The sphere of authority that YHWH gave to Yeshua and that we are sharing in encompasses the heaven and the earth; that was why he prayed: thy kingdom come, they will be done on earth as it is in heaven. (Matthew 6:9). While the will of YHWH is still being done on earth, there are yet areas where the earth is not catching up.

Welfare

Heaven's welfare program is unequaled and unparalleled in the entire world, nothing like it. For I know the thoughts I think towards you, says the Lord, thought of welfare and of prosperity, thought to settle you and to increase you. (See Jeremiah 29:11) No government on earth can ever think that much of its citizenries. So comprehensive and compact is this program that there is:

No poverty. No hunger. No lack, there. YHWH sees to the need of ten thousands of His saints at the snap of His finger; He supplies all of their need according to His riches in glory by the

Messiah, Yeshua. Nothing equals it. Heaven's welfare package is abundance. (See Isaiah 65:17-25 and 2 Cor. 8:9)

Healthcare

Our health need has been provided for by the cross of Yahshua, all sicknesses dealt with and all diseases suffered for and put away. Our health insured by the blood of His cross-forever settled in heaven and on earth. There is no need for healthcare policies and bills, it has been passed and it is eternally sealed by the token of the sacrifice-blood of Yahshua, in that we do not have to go for routine checkups and treatment but just take in the cure and stay with it. Heaven's is the order, the earth is copying.

We receive cures not treatments. Every drop of blood that fell from the body of the crucified Nazarene is the cure; every stripe that landed on his lacerated body brought us healing. We do not need to go checking and begging and advocating; all we need is to reach out and take the cure: "For by the wound of Yahshua we are cured."

Housing

No lack, no want, no sicknesses and no housing need. YHWH's housing scheme has been settled in eternity; houses and streets made of gold, mansions built with diamond and heaven's most precious stones, like those that went into the making of Lucifer as described in Ezekiel 28; what could be better? No overpopulation, no slums, no low income settlement; no mortgages and foreclosures, all planned out by the Ministry of Works and Housing of the kingdom of YHWH.

The Father's house: In the shadow of the almighty

We have it all made in the Kingdom, the shadow of the almighty, His great presence is house to all who come and stay. To all who believe in the sacrifice of the Son of YHWH and respond with a yes to it.

There we belong, no weeping, no sorrow there, no tenancy there, all are home, landlord and landladies to YHWH's real estate for time and for eternity. Just think about the worries that are lifted off one's mind when the burden of rent renewal is removed by way of one being able to own his or her own property in our world. Heaven is much more rewarding and beautiful.

Companionship

I will never leave you nor forsake you, for lo I am with you always even unto the end of the age, is the great remark that launches Joshua and the apostles into their promised land. YHWH has not changed. The Father is our friend and companion, or companion for life. We live with Him in us and with us, we are encompassed and surrounded by His love and presence, that which the angels pride over.

He is with us when we go out and when we come back, when we sit down, lie down to sleep, when we are eating and drinking. He is our eternal companion.

Heaven is all comfort because of the glory of YHWH's presence and that is what we are called to enjoy-to share in the glory and virtue of Yahshua. We are not alone, the Holy Spirit is in us, the Father is with us, the Son is with us through His imperial name; the innumerable company of angels are on our side, holy saints who have gone to glory stand on the grandstands of heaven, watching and applauding our progress; we have the whole unseen holy world to our side. YHWH is for us and if YHWH be for us who can be against us (See Joshua 1:5, Matthew 28:20, Hebrews 12:22 and Romans 8:31)

Kingdom citizens are family

We are citizens of the kingdom, we are family. "For our citizenship is in heaven, from which we also eagerly wait for the Savior, the Lord Yeshua the Messiah," (Philippians 3:20)

The Father's pride is His family; we are members of the family and household of YHWH. Yeshua is the eldest Son of the family, His name is the family name, we are a nucleus, he is the family lawyer and all the graces of the wealthiest and richest family in the universe is on us. Let us go for it. (See Ephesians. 2:19 and Galatians 6:10)

Justice

The foundation of the kingdom and throne of YHWH is righteousness and justice (Psalm 89:14 and 97:2). The Scripture says to ascribe ye greatness unto our YHWH. He is the Rock, his work is perfect: for all his ways are judgment: a YHWH of truth and without iniquity, just and right is he. (Deuteronomy 32:3-4, KJV). YHWH is a just YHWH, there is no partiality with him, and there are no favorites in his courts; to Him, what is good for the goose is also good for the gander.

He is the lawgiver and interpreter, His advocacy is right and unbending. No man is bigger than His orders and no offender is too big to be punished by Him, no one can influence His judgment and no one can bend his rule. His laws are fixed and clear, even the commonest among people can read and understand, only one lawyer is required, Yeshua of Nazareth, the righteous.

The rich are not considered above the poor in His court and anybody can be arraigned before Him. His judgments are trusted and founded, no one can question it. (See Romans 11:33)

Everyone in Heaven and Earth receives just penalty as directed by YHWH. The justices of YHWH are just and right, He does not measure out punishment and rewards arbitrarily and no one can influence his ruling. Once His court passes judgment, it is accurate and impartial. There are no creations of His, whether in heaven and on earth, whether angels, demons and humans that do not receive due recompense as ordered by his court. Once the court has passed its ruling, you can be sure it is just and no one can evade it.

A compassionate and caring King

In our kingdom is a King who sits at the helm of affairs, kindness and compassionate depict His nature and character. He is benevolent, generous and of a large heart. For every good gift and every perfect gift is from above, and comes down from the Father of lights, with whom there is no variation or shadow of turning. (James 1:17 and verse 5)

His liberality is such that He causes the sun to shine on the good and the bad, His rain to fall on the righteous and the unrighteous, his heaven to give light on both his children and even on the subjects of his enemy. There is no holding back of His grace and benevolence, He so lavishes His love on His children that He doesn't even mind if others-outside of His kingdom come for a feel of it.

There is no area of need his grace does not cover for time and for eternity, He cares, the Bible says, He willingly gives of His abundance on all those that call and wait on Him. (See 1 Peter 5:7)

He supplies your needs and your wants

There are no needs that exist in the kingdom, because the loving caring Father supplies them accordingly; the need for wisdom, He will supply, be it ability, knowledge, husband, children, finances, deliverance, healing, guidance and even down to your bathing soap, He does supply according to His riches in glory by the Messiah Yeshua. There is no lack with YHWH, there are no shortages with Him, there is no scarcity in His kingdom, all the goods and merchandise of the kingdom are abundantly subsidized by the blood of the Lamb and in the name of Yeshua one can have and enjoy as many one wishes any day and anytime. His provision is for all.

The strongest military

Talk about military intelligence and might; no nation on earth equals that of our kingdom. Talk about sophistication, no army is like it; in number, the most populated nation on earth does not come close to it. One of His lieutenants can destroy over 180,000 soldiers in one night, I mean not with tanks and bombs, but just by sheer massacre. (See 2 Kings 19:35)

The Scripture talks about ten thousands and thousands of YHWH's angels, myriads of angelic intelligence and marshals that no nation can withstand or equal. It is the strongest in the universe. (See Revelation 5:11)

The angelic military with our Father as commander in Chief

Bless the LORD, you His angels, who excel in strength, who do His word, heeding the voice of His word. Bless the LORD, all you His hosts, you ministers of His, who do His pleasure. (Psalm 103:20-21) Do you think that I cannot now pray to My Father, and He will provide Me with more than twelve legions of angels? (Matthew 26:53)

YHWH's hosts are billions and billions of angels with Him at the head of the command. They carry out His orders without hesitation and without question. His word is a law for them and they do it without reservation. All the might of Satan and his intelligence is no match for it, and never can be.

The Fruits of the spirit (no conflict, no hatred, no discord, etc.)

There are no citizens of any nation that don't connect with each other by way of relationships. But at best there are still hinges, cheating, deception and pride. But in the kingdom of YHWH, it is not so. There are no competitions there; therefore there is no jealousy, no hatred and no conflict.

The operations of the kingdom are for the common good of all and no one claims anything as his own: "And of Zion it will be said, "This one and that one were born in her; and the Most High Himself shall establish her." The LORD will record, When He registers the people: "This one was born there." (Psalm 87:5-6)

Talk about love, joy and peace, that's what you will see and get in the kingdom; talk about gentleness, goodness, and self-control, these are the virtues and pride of the citizenries of the nation of heaven. Patience, faithfulness and kindness are all hallmark of the kingdom. What you cannot find in YHWH, cannot be found among the citizens of the kingdom.

Visitors To Heaven Come Back Raving

All those who are on Earth that have ever even glimpsed at Heaven have been awed and desire to immigrate there. If Yeshua is your King, you should be visiting Heaven regularly; learning of its many treasures. There is always something new to find and explore in Heaven. Our Father is not done creating, and no one has been able to entirely explore everything that He has created. The ratio of satisfaction from citizens is 100%; no one desires to leave and everyone is full of joy. The per capita is uncountable--complete abundance is accessible to each member. Education is complete and the Father has assigned seven spirits to train you to your fullness, rather than the fragmented ideas of Earth's inhabitants or education systems (more on this in later chapters). Agriculture and nutrition is not a problem in Heaven because the King provides the nutrients that each citizen needs to include their intake of virtues. Healthcare is not needed because the King provides cures prior to entrance into Heaven. Natural resources are plentiful. Pollution is not possible. All relationships are successful. Unemployment is not a factor because no one works to attain sustenance, rather, they are always experiencing joy and excitement praising the Lord, and exploring the depths of the Heavens. There are no language barriers or segregation. Do you understand? ANY problem that can be experienced on the Earth finds its solution in Heaven, and you can enter at your liberty because of Yeshua. Heaven has reigned and been the happiest and most powerful kingdom from the beginning of the world, and will continue to be eternally. If the kings of the Earth have access to Heaven, they can import ideas, resources, and other solutions that can drastically transform their kingdoms.

The only program on earth that is fair is that of YHWH, because YHWH runs his program His way. YHWH's word is infallible, by His Spirit and through the instrumentality of humans; yet even at that, no man is indispensable. He puts down one and raises another. But the world's ways are not like that. Faulty programs on the foundation of wrong ideologies and philosophies, produce an unstable system and economy. What do you make of a blind leading the blind? They will both fall into the ditch. (See Matthew 15:14) The only sure-to-work plan is the very word of the Lord which is in it-self SURE. (2 Peter 1:19)

CHAPTER FIVE

BE STRONG IN SPIRITUAL SELF-DEFENSE

"James tells us there are four sources of 'wisdom' you can be listening to: wisdom from above (heavenly wisdom), earthly wisdom, natural wisdom, and demonic wisdom (James 3:15). Which of those are you resonating with? Who or what are you coming into agreement with? Because when you start to agree with the frequency of heaven, when you start to with the heart of YHWH, then heaven comes to earth through your life."
- Mike Parsons

The Story of Jennifer and Jose

Jennifer was a powerful woman of YHWH. She hosted crusades within low income neighborhoods to teach people how Yeshua is the solution to their every need. She was known for leading people to miracles, signs, wonders, and supernatural supply from Heaven. In her crusade in Chicago, Illinois, many people arrived. She spoke and offered people the opportunity to become citizens of Heaven, and not one person responded.

She began praying and YHWH told her that more than half of those that arrived were heavy into occult practices. Jennifer decided to fast and to gather a team of intercessors to pray before, during, and after the crusade. She said, "My defense was weak last night and we have to arm up".

Jose was a powerful priest of Voodoo. He maintained a spiritual map of his area. He had markings to identify where Christian activity was taking place, and he stayed very conscious of who was stepping into his territory. He would do séances, ceremonies, and commune with the devil all night long. He would say, "Curse them. Make them drop dead. Make their crusade and their whole business fail!" He made his income from killings that he would perform merely by placing a magic spell on someone. People would come to him anytime they envied another person for their husband or their opportunity, when they wanted to create hatred, discord, or other evils in the lives of others. He would do his spell and people would die within days. Businesses would go bankrupt. Families would fall apart. Powerless and immature Christians would backslide and never return.

Jose found out Jennifer was coming to his area. He intended to kill her with his spells. He said, "Chicago does not need her God. I want her dead!" He bought a coffin, bought animals for blood sacrifices, placed her picture in the coffin, drank the blood, and prayed to the devil all night long without eating. He sent numerous demons to frustrate her mission and create chaos in her mind, family, and sickness in her body. When the demons would return, he asked, "Is she dead yet?" They said, "We could not touch her. There is blood all over her and we cannot penetrate the blood."

Jose went to the first day of Jennifer's crusade with hopes to supernaturally kill her, but he was unsuccessful. He was able to distract the minds of her audience and caused no one to receive the gift of salvation.

When Jennifer and Jose arrived for the second day of the crusade, the intercessors prayed, and announced in the spiritual realm that not only would people be saved and healed, but the enemy would be plundered. Thousands were saved that day and the demons operating with Jose fled. He was left alone and regained possession of his body and soul. Void of demonic advice, Jose began to think, "Who is this power that is stronger than those that I summon? I want access to the kingdom that is more powerful than the one that I knew before." Jose chose to receive Yeshua as his King and his life drastically changed. He experienced demonic attacks for two months following his conversion because the devil demanded his return, but with the power of YHWH, he sent the devil in flight. Rather than being powerful for the kingdom in darkness, he became a righteous man of YHWH with a recognized and admirable reputation. He was an eye-opener for others enslaved by the kingdom in darkness, and he prospered in his business and family.

Defend yourself with your armor

With any altercation, adults and babies alike understand the importance of defending one's self. Even when something as small as an insect comes close to a person's face, most people wave their hands in attempts to ward it off. Surprisingly, the kingdom in darkness swarms closer than any insect, and most people are ill-prepared to ward them off. YHWH has prepared each and every one of us, so that we do not have to be shot at, but rather, we can overtake the enemy by force. Let's discuss your armor in spiritual self-defense:

Put on your shield of faith

On the Earth, you will be exposed to many things, but you must be mindful that your reality is created spiritually first. Faith is exercised in more than one way; it is a shield to dodge arrows, but it also a form of currency which purchases imports from Heaven to Earth. It's up to you to address matters with the King; rather than to place your hope in another physical "treatment". He is the only cure. When something physically defies His promise or His covenant written to you in His word, you put up your shield of faith; exercising your "No!" power. When statistics, doubt, or fear raise flags of opposition, you say, "No! The King of Heaven has said…" or you declare the decree as written in the Bible, saying, "It is written…". Your faith can be used to move mountains amongst other things, but there are some things that cannot be purchased by your faith, rather, you will have to be anointed by the king for some, while for others, you will have to enter the glory or the presence of YHWH to receive them (we will discuss this concept more later).

As you walk in obedience and submission, YHWH will give you the responsibility to exemplify good stewardship with more. In other words, as you steward well, he will enlarge your territory. For this reason, Yeshua said, "Those who have, more will be given to them. Those who do not have, even what they have will be taken away". Exercise the ability you have with your faith interacting with the power of YHWH; this alone can liberate others with evidence of miracles, signs, and wonders. As you show yourself as an approved ambassador, you will be given gifts (increased revelation, prophesy, discerning of spirits, a heavenly tongue, and many more), you will be given an increased anointing, and the glory of

YHWH will be apparent to you everywhere you go.

The glory is a place; not a physical place, but rather a spiritual place. The glory is a dimension. Similar to the dimensions of the Earth's atmosphere--composed of exosphere, thermosphere, mesosphere, stratosphere, and troposphere--there are also dimensions preceding the presence of YHWH. You first must pass thru the dimensions of faith past, "I think" to "I know" then thru the anointing, then thru the glory. Every dimension for entry into the presence is indescribable, but when you get past the dimensions of your own effort (those of Faith and Anointing) to those where YHWH is solely at work (the dimensions of glory and His presence), that is where the unimaginable takes place.

The Gospel of Peace

Moses, Elijah, Elisha, Yeshua, the disciples and others have shown you the power that is accessible to you by aligning with the laws of Heaven. Their testimonies were not written to confine YHWH, but to reveal Him. The things written of should be increased in the lives of believers today. Unlike Elijah and Moses who fought their battles physically, you have been given increased authority by the resurrection power of Yeshua. Yes, it is true Yeshua died, which to some may appear he lost if you stop there, but that is not the end of the story, it continues. He descended to Sheol (the place where dead souls rest), he entered two regions there (as mentioned in the parable of the rich man and Lazarus). He entered the region of torment (where unbelievers await judgment) and Abraham's bosom (where the righteous awaited the completion of the Messiah's salvation plan) (Luke 16:19-31). He experienced the torment for our sake, he experienced separation (the inability to speak to or commune with YHWH), an atmosphere of complete (100%) evil, He endured the wrath of YHWH, took the keys from Satan, trampled him under his feet by ascending from the pits of hell and raising from the dead. Not only did he raise from the dead, but he also brought many others with him (See Matthew 27:52-53 for an eyewitness testimony).

YHWH will give you the Holy Spirit to the same degree which you jealously guard it. Live your life to host His presence. Do not develop your intimacy with YHWH for the sake of a profession; rather your intimacy should be based on just a mere desire to be with Him. Delight in His presence just for His presence's sake. What you're most aware of emanates from you.

When Yeshua walked amongst a crowd, a woman with the issue of blood placed her faith in the idea that if she simply touched his garment, she would be made whole. When a person is focused on fear, their fear emanates from them. When a person is full of doubt, their doubt can be felt in the atmosphere. Similarly, when a person is continually focused on the Holy Spirit, even their shadows and garments can bring healing to those around them. The dove always looks for somewhere to rest.

Physical laws the Earth and its inhabitants must abide by can be transcended by tapping into the supernatural realm. Unfortunately, in the present, occultists and Occultists exercise defiance against the natural laws by tapping into the supernatural laws of the kingdom in darkness, but you do not seek YHWH to transcend physical barriers. You name it, He can do it. You read it in His word, He can create and surpass it. Even more, He can create unimaginable things. The gospel of peace is the greatest medicine; it provides your instructions for how to attain your Kingdom benefits, how to transform bad into good, and how to turn heartache into laughter.

Therefore just as He overcame all things (sickness, disease, mental anguish, hatred, rejection, pain, curses, death, and all other evils imaginable), He has given you His signet ring (His stamp of authority) for you trample Satan and his army underfoot, and take back territory he has unlawful possession of (we will discuss this more in depth later). YHWH can do greater than He has revealed prior. When the Kingdom is manifested, peace is inevitable. Take with you the gospel of peace everywhere you go!

Helmet of Salvation

Your enemy will constantly throw arrows; many of which will be directed at your mind. The kingdom in darkness attempts to import doubt and export faith; this is their primary strategy. As a result of Adam's surrender of his birthright, all were born with a sinful nature, and with poorly trained and low voltage Ambassadors, the Earth is becoming a place of deeper and deeper darkness. Discernment is a gift few have requested from the Kingdom of Heaven, therefore most people allow the penetration of enemy arrows because they lack the discernment to see, identify, or defend themselves from them. Right and wrong are very difficult to identify for most. Satan has tried with all of his effort to neutralize the truth, and steer you to what's wrong. For this reason, the wisest man of all time, King Solomon said we should ask above all things for the ability to discern right from wrong. Your helmet of salvation is padded with discernment, insight, and is seamless at guarding you from attacks to your mind.

Salvation means "preservation or deliverance from ruin, loss, or harm". With your helmet on, you will be protected from the enemy's attempts to withdraw things from your mind, from their attempts to add to your mind, or when they attempt to be destructive to your assets there. Protect your memory, the Truth, your revealed secrets, amongst your other assets by placing your helmet of salvation on. Your helmet will give you the ability to be defended from attacks in the dark, murky, environment of the Earth, so keep it on!

Your belt of truth

The Bible speaks of the belt to be used as a tool to enable you to move with haste, to hold clothing in place, to carry mission-essential items (such as water or weaponry), and as a sign of honor. The belt enables you to move with haste because you don't have to worry yourself with your garments falling, and you don't have to gather all of your belongings because the belt has placed them in a reachable location where you can quickly respond to attacks. When your belt is worn, you do not place yourself at risk by putting weaponry or other necessities down, and enabling the enemy when he steals your tools.

When I was in the military, I remember seeing people get in trouble for putting down their weapons (even in practice exercises where the weaponry was fake). We were taught the weaponry was of high value to the military, it was expensive, and when they are put down, it puts the entire country in harm's way. Accordingly, a person who puts their weapon down was not simply the recipient of a pat on the hand. Rather, they were given severe disciplinary action. Those of higher rank had greater access, and if they were to put their weapons down, very severe disciplinary action takes place because a larger message is sent off. Imagine, if a commander of 10,000 military personnel nonchalantly places his weapon down (regardless of reason). It sends the message that the entire force may be poorly trained, low skilled, or careless.

Similar to my military experience, the belt of truth holds a high value to the Kingdom of Heaven, and as an ambassador of Yahshua, it needs to hold the same value to you. The Truth is the single ingredient that holds the functions of our world together, and if any of them were compromised, creation would be nonexistent. Yeshua, the creator of eternity, said, "I am the way, the Truth, and the Life." We know His blood purchased access to eternity for the entire Earth's population and those who resided in Sheol. Accordingly, if we are instructed to wear this same truth on us at all times, we must understand the value in what we are wearing. If trendy clothing is guarded and esteemed, how much more, the belt of truth? Don't take it off!

When your weapon is around your waist, it is in close proximity to your hands, and when an attacker proceeds, you can respond to grab your weapon in milliseconds or less (depending on your skill level and practice). Truth is IMPORTANT! When you sense the enemy approaching or when arrows of deceit aim in your direction, you should be able to respond quickly with truth. When you are instructed to move from location to location, truth should be amongst the primary necessities on your being. Your belt of truth also serves as a symbol of allegiance and honor to the Kingdom for which you stand. As Americans place their left hands over their hearts to say, "I pledge allegiance to the flag of the United States of America". Your garment expresses the same allegiance; it is a mark of loyalty, submission, and obedience. In addition, the belt of truth maintains the placement of the Sword of the Spirit on your being. Keep your belt on, so that when the enemy attempts to overtake you, you can respond with haste.

Sword of the Spirit

Swords inflate or deflate in value and use depending on the sharpness of the blade. A sharp blade can be used to overtake whole armies, while contrarily, a dull blade can be an army's demise. In historic battles, the sword was the primary weapon used to destroy an enemy. Even after years of weapon exploration, the sword is amongst the most vicious weapons. Unlike a bullet that simply makes a small hole thru the body cavities, the sword slices limbs off, carves organs out, or even, cuts off the head. Swords are typically used to pierce vital organs and kill an enemy, but success can only be accomplished with passion and skill.

Bone marrow is a soft, spongy substance that fills the inner cavity of the bones; where the blood is produced. To harvest bone marrow, typically, surgeons (physicians with years of practice) have to give the patient anesthesia to help with pain, they use very sharp needles that penetrate thru the skin into the bone, and separate the bone from the marrow. Even with much skill and expertise, only the hip bones or the sternum are typically used to harvest marrow. Joints, would be increasingly difficult to harvest marrow.

Unlike any other sword known to man, the Sword of the Spirit is said to be so sharp and precise it can separate joints from marrow! It also has the ability to divide soul and spirit, and judge thoughts and attitudes of the heart (Hebrews 4:12). The sword of the spirit has greater capability than any other sword known to man, and is a tool given only to those adherents to the New Testament. In his teaching called, *Identifying the Strongman*, Apostle Renny Mclean talked about the difference in the authority of those alive during the Old Testament and the New Testament. He said in the Old Testament, believers were not given the ability to separate soul from spirit, therefore people had to be killed because of the presence of a demon within them. However, in the New Testament, scripture says the weapons of our warfare are not carnal. 2 Corinthians 10:3-5 says, *"For though we walk in the flesh, we do not war according to the flesh. 4 For the weapons of our warfare are not carnal but mighty in YHWH for pulling down strongholds, 5 casting down arguments and every high thing that exalts itself against the knowledge of YHWH, bringing every thought into captivity to the obedience of Yahshua"*. Our battles are fought spiritually (as demonstrated by Yeshua thru casting out demons and fighting with the Word of YHWH) rather than physically (as demonstrated by YHWH's command and exercised by his forefather David). The exercise of New Testament authority is asserted thru the mouth, quoting the pure words of YHWH. Our sword gives us the ability to discern the voices that we hear in our heads and the identity of the Holy Spirit, angels, demons or a dictatorship of the flesh affecting those around us. Therefore, read your word--sharpening your access to its content--, and gain skill in using it to rebut the attacks of the enemy!

Breastplate of righteousness

Of all body extremities, your head and your chest are the two that that have the greatest effect on the livelihood of the entire body. When enemy fire is targeted at either of these extremities, it is deadly! The head commands the entire mission of life thru mission-essential thoughts while the chest pumps the most essential nutrients to support and fulfill the mission.

For Earthly militaries, the operations are spread out. Kitchens are downwind of bathrooms, armories are not located with publicity departments, and intelligence is typically the most isolated of them all. While spread apart, each operation must work coherently for the mission to succeed, but in spite of it all; some operations (such as medical, intelligence, and infantry) are the lifeblood of a military. If an enemy wants to wipe out its opponents, they know to aim for the head and the chest of the person's body, and of the entire operation.

Similarly, Satan's mission is to kill you, so he instructs his army to aim at the head and chest of your body, and the head and chest of what he knows about your entire life operation. He aims to take you out!

Righteousness can only be achieved by crucifying self. Righteousness is not done for anyone else, but simply for your own protection; it is your choice to spend eternity in glory. Yeshua forsook his will, bore the sins of the world, the torment, the diseases, the rejection, the pain, and transcended the ability of Satan to ensnare us with that by raising from the dead victoriously. Afterwards, he assigned you to have authority to do the same. When you come in contact with your will which is defiant by natural birth, you must crucify it, and align with Yahshua. This means when you have been instructed to do something to reach your next assigned spiritual location, despite your feelings, your desires, or the advice of others, you crucify Self, and align with Yahshua. Crucifying your will protect you. It maintains the integrity of your operation. If you take of your breastplate of righteousness, you risk the possibility of a strike on your livelihood with consequences of instant spiritual (and possibly physical) death.

When the enemy aims your way or even attacks the livelihood of your mission, the breastplate of righteousness will not enable him to succeed. 100% of the time, your breastplate of righteousness will guard your chest cavity (the storehouse of your most needed life nutrients) from enemy force. Scientists say the average person can only live 3 minutes without air, they can lose no more than 40% of their blood supply, and their heart cannot stop for more than 3 minutes. With this being said, a person who has been struck in either the head (with thoughts of destruction) or the chest (with a curse that separates them from revelation and communion with YHWH or man) is in critical danger.

Take Authority of Your Gates

In wartime, every nation knows to protect their gates because if an enemy steps into their gates, he can plunder their town. You are in war and you must protect the gates of your body, soul, spirit, and the Glory of YHWH that emanates from the inside of you. In his book, *The Realms of the Kingdom Volume 1*, Ian Clayton details the gates of each dimension of your being. Some of the gates that

Ian wrote of are listed below:

Your Body: The Gates To Your Soul - Your Outer Court
- Eyes
- Ears
- Nose
- Mouth
- Sense of Touch

Your Soul: The Gates To Your Spirit - Your Inner Court
- Prayer
- Worship
- Reverence
- Fear of YHWH
- Praise
- Choices
- Will
- Imagination

Your Spirit: The Gate To The Glory of YHWH
- First Love

Each of your gates must be well guarded, and you must live from the inside out; from the glory inside of you to the glory that will rest on you from Heaven. From the intimate love of YHWH, you should make your choices, your will should be reflective of your first love, your worship will pour from the inside, your conversation, and what you entertain should all flow from the inside. You must crucify your soul with all of its fleshly desires, and crave the Glory of YHWH. When the glory overshadows your Spirit and your flesh, and body are in submission to the glory; you will be able to access Heaven and all of its abundance. Anything unclean about you will be burned away by the glorious fire of YHWH, but you must first change your paradigm from living from the outside in, and live from and in the Spirit.

Exercise

1. Sit down with Deuteronomy 28 and read about the blessings and the curses of YHWH

2. Be honest with yourself and write down which blessings you have access to and which curses plague you. Identify the areas that the curse has affected you.

3. Ask YHWH, "How did this curse fall on me?"

4. Restore sanctity and clarity to your borders. Repent for whichever part you or your forefathers played in the enemy having access to your authorized territory.

5. Identify how the enemy is attempting to commit terrorism outside of your borders. Ask YHWH, "Make clear to me right and wrong, so I can make just decisions".

CHAPTER SIX

PLUNDER THE ENEMY!

Destiny was a young single mother. In high school, she met a young guy who she thought she would spend the rest of her life with. He had a lot of interest in Destiny, but not the proper understanding of his mandate as a Kingdom man. They had two children together. One named Rock and one named Desiree. Rock was very rebellious. Whenever he was asked to do something, he would sigh and retaliate with excuses.

Desiree was very disorganized and destructive to the things that were purchased for her. When she got new clothes, she would throw them on the floor. Her room was completely disorganized and her belongings did not last long because she did not care for them properly.

Destiny was so concentrated on her work she did not make time to confront her children when they did things wrong. Their behavior got to a point where she no longer felt capable of correcting them. The family finances would come and go, they had a bad reputation for poor time management, hygiene, and cleanliness. Healthy food was not affordable because they had to purchase items unnecessarily due to poor organization and preservation habits, so each of them had health problems. They were overweight and undernourished; each having sickness many times per month. Destiny desperately wanted a solution.

How To Get Spiritual Intelligence About the Enemy's Tactical Work

Even with an outstanding running back and offense, without defense, you will lose the game. The Bible tells us the spiritual enemy comes to steal, kill, and destroy, but Yeshua came that we should have life to the full (John 10:10). A person or group that attempts to steal, kill, or destroy from another country is considered a terrorist. For many people, they are not able to identify the attacks of the enemy.

Destiny's joy was being stolen by her ongoing disputes with her children. Her time was stolen by her disorganization, the excessive amount of time that she would spend searching for things, and her reputation was damaged as a result. Her family lost their unity because of rebellion, bad habits, and their damaged reputation. "A good name is more desirable than great riches; to be esteemed is better than silver or gold." A reputation is more valuable than currency; it is a source and a form of wealth. So the enemy had stolen many very valuable things from Destiny and her lineage.

Identify Spiritual Terrorism

Terrorists are typically identified thru the process of military intelligence. Military.org says, "Military intelligence is information needed to plan for our national defense. Knowledge of the number, location, and tactics of enemy forces and potential battle areas is needed to develop military plans. To gather information, the services rely on aerial photographs, electronic monitoring using radar, satellites and sensitive radios, and human observation.

Intelligence specialists gather and study the information required to design defense plans and tactics."

A collection of intelligence is given to the leader of the United States every day so he can make wise decisions about the future of the country. Things like Iran gaining access to more plutonium or uranium (resources used for nuclear warfare) are important bits of insight for a government leader because they enable him to brace the country and prepare a strategy for success. As a result of military intelligence, presidents discuss their insight with advisers and other government diplomats to collectively create a strategy to protect and defend the territory they have given authority over.

Without military intelligence, country's leaders would not be prepared with vital insight to pre-plan based on a clear view of the world at large. They would not be able to defend and protect the country, and even worse, they would not be able to identify the enemy. On extreme cases, countries' borders are breached, and they are not aware because military intelligence officials have not identified the terrorist as an enemy, or they are so deceived they believe what is meant to harm them is for good.

Grow in Discerning of Spirits

Similarly, you have been given authority over territories, and you need intelligence to identify the enemy attacks within your realm of dominion. One such area of your dominion is your mind, another is your connections, and another is your finances, your property, your prophetic utterances, and your revelation. Most "Christian" people do not have a renewed mind. They are not intentional in their spiritual walk, and therefore, when the enemy attacks, they are unable to separate him from their own voice or even worse, they cannot discern the enemy's voice from YHWH. Is this you?

The enemy's purpose is to steal, kill, and destroy. He wants to export your peace, your joy, your love, and the other fruits of the Spirit, sever your communion with YHWH, and send you astray dying without your birthright of eternity. He wants to import lies, tolerance, complacency, and other forms of deception. You can identify his voice when you analyze the fruit of his words. For example, if a husband and wife disagree, he may compromise the conversation by planting lies like, "your husband doesn't even care how you feel. You should do something to him, so he can know how it feels to hurt you". His words are intended to increase hatred, hostility, isolation, and transfer your birthright to him and his fallen angels. You need to begin identifying his voice, and write down when he attempts to commit acts of terrorism.

The voice of YHWH will multiply you, expand you, and provides supernatural insight that positively affects you, those around you, and His kingdom. He is your Commander, the Creator of your mission, and the Ally that laid His son down, so that you could live. When you are low on resources, you import them from the Kingdom of YHWH. You need to identify His voice to give Him His pay (your praise) for your resources (all of your needs being met).

If you do not do daily intelligence to create a continual strategy to overcome the attacks, how will you identify when you are not experiencing the Kingdom of Heaven in areas of your life? How will you create a strategy to prevail in battles that you are currently facing or ones that are to come? How will you overcome (or instruct them to overcome) the battles that plague your children, your spouse, your other family members, your community, your city, or your nation?

Bold statement…"Just like a country that lacks intelligence is bound to fail. A person who lacks intelligence is also bound to fail."

You better believe the enemy has precise intelligence on you. He knows when you have accessed Heaven, he sends his army to spy and find out if you are spending time in your prayer closet, and he has created a strategy to reel you back in. Are you as prepared as he is to take complete possession of your mind, your family, your property, and all else the enemy attempts to steal? It's your possession, and the battle is real. When you have shown the ability to walk with a renewed mind; one uncompromised by the prevailing trends and thought patterns of your time, and you present yourself as a peculiar priest, then you can pray the prayer of Jabez because you have demonstrated good stewardship.

Go Before The Courts Of YHWH

The world's justice systems are not always fair. They are corrupt and not always fair because they are run and interpreted by humans who themselves are with faults. Most people (even attorneys and judges) dread going to man-made courts, but contrarily, King David said of the court of Heaven "Better is one day in your courts than one thousand elsewhere". Isn't that shocking? As a King in one of the most documented nations of the world, he would say he would rather spend 1 day in court than one thousand anywhere else?! Court in Heaven MUST be awesome!

Proverbs 19:36 says you cannot have an honest system of judgement aside from YHWH. It says, "Honest scales and balances belong to the Lord; all the weights in the bag are of his making." You cannot accurately measure time, volume, length, weight, hearts, attitudes, lies and truth, right and wrong, or anything else without the help of YHWH. There is no stability in systems other than those that YHWH put in place. For example, any time paper money has been put into place, the government system has always collapsed. YHWH gave each person goods, talents, skills, and revelation as currency. When we exchange talents, goods, services, skills, and revelation, we have an efficient economy. When we place man-made systems of measurement, they do not last long in comparison to the works of YHWH. You need the scales of YHWH for stability and lasting success. The gifts given by YHWH convert to every currency and every time period because He transcends it all and is the author.

No person that is weak has a right to crucify one that is weak also, but that is the world's way. Not so with our kingdom, we are representative of a just ruler and judge-Yeshua the Messiah, the righteous. (See James 4:12) The Bible tells you, you assuredly receive justice from the throne of YHWH when you:

- Take your case against the courts of YHWH

- Plead guilty rather than arguing with the accuser.

Short explanation for those of you reading saying, "Why should I plead guilty for something that I did not do?": Your DNA record tracks the wrongs of you and your lineage all the way back to Adam. Knowing this, the accuser accuses you for things beyond your time on Earth

- Repent to the King

- Pay the debt with the blood of Yeshua

The Judge will judge fairly, He will blot out your transgressions, ensure justice if you have been wrongfully accused, and ensure retroactive pay. We lose our cases and reap injustice simply because we do not show up. Yeshua said:

"Settle matters quickly with your adversary who is taking you to court. Do it while you are still together on the way, or your adversary may hand you over to the judge, and the judge may hand you over to the officer, and you may be thrown into prison. Truly I tell you, you will not get out until you have paid the last penny." (Matthew 5:24-26)

Exercise

Write down the breaches of the enemy, the full blown attacks of the enemy, his movement in the lives around you, and create a strategy to place increased borders and combat each of his moves.

Take a moment now to write down:

- The fruits of your flesh that are manifesting

- The familiar spirits that you hear

- Write the manifestations that oppose YHWH's will in your body (sickness, disease, acne, poor eyesight, etc.)

- Write down accusations that people have made against you

- Fees that you've been charged that you shouldn't

- Debts that you owe

- Write down opposites to YHWH's will in your DNA record (birth defects from your lineage, genetic habits, attitudes, curses, etc.)

- Write down any areas where you sense lack

Take this list before the throne of YHWH. Begin by praising YHWH. Enter His gates with thanksgiving, and his courts with praise (Psalms 100). Request that YHWH blot out all of these markings from your records and your lineage. Take your judicial papers with all of the cancelled debts and continue to affirm that the King has made you FREE! Notify time saying, "The balance on this debt is erased now!". Notify your body saying, "The sickness or defect is gone now!". Be Free in Yeshua' name!

Find a promise of YHWH for each breach, attack, or plan of the enemy, meditate and pray the scripture.

Go to the court of YHWH. David said one day in the court of YHWH is better than one thousand anywhere else. Do you know why? His heir caused us to always win in court. We repent, pay our court fees and debts with the blood of Yeshua, and our sins are acquitted! You plunder the enemy every time you enter the court with the plan to repent of the accusations against you. Confess, and watch the righteous Judge assign judiciary papers that release you from the liens the kingdom in darkness has placed on your blessings. Yeshua will advocate for you in court as your high priest. When you ask, our Father will grant you the necessary angels to ensure that your gates are protected in the future. He will delete the record of wrong captured in your DNA, and plunder what the enemy has wrongfully taken from you. Assign angels to breach areas and to combat plans of the enemy. Isn't that awesome? You may be wondering, "How do I get to the court?" David gave instructions in Psalms 100:4 saying, "Enter his gates with thanksgiving and his courts with praise; give thanks to him and praise his name."

Our judicial system is perfect and the fairest in the world; no spiritual being or physical being can get away with injustice in Heaven's courts, the just judge with His omniscience always knows. For He punishes and rewards every person according to what he or she has done. (Hebrews 4:12-13)

CHAPTER SEVEN

BE STRONG IN OFFENSIVE SPIRITUAL WARFARE TACTICS

The Story Of Two Mighty Men In Offense

Elijah was a man of YHWH. He was known for transcending natural laws and excelling in offensive spiritual warfare tactics. He stopped the rain from pouring for three years as a rebuke for those who submitted to the kingdom in darkness. He always maintained a strong defensive strategy through prayer, fasting, and communing with YHWH. Beyond defense, he plundered the enemy, sent them fleeing, and enlarged the territory for the Kingdom of Heaven.

On one particular occasion, Elijah was filled with holy rage. Evil was increasing in his area, and prophets of YHWH were being killed. Elijah presented a challenge to the occultists saying:

"How long will you go limping with two different opinions? If the Lord is God, follow him; but if Baal, then follow him." The people did not answer him a word. Then Elijah said to the people, "I, even I only, am left a prophet of the Lord; but Baal's prophets number four hundred fifty. Let two bulls be given to us; let them choose one bull for themselves, cut it in pieces, and lay it on the wood, but put no fire to it; I will prepare the other bull and lay it on the wood, but put no fire to it. Then you call on the name of your god and I will call on the name of the YHWH; the god who answers by fire is indeed God." (1 Kings 18: 21-24)

They were not able to keep up with the challenge and prove their power was greater than the power of YHWH, so Elijah slew the men.

Mattathias experienced a similar challenge. Under Greek rule, evil became heightened near his camp. The King knew he had a prestigious reputation among many people, so they attempted to create an alliance with him saying:

"You are a leader, honored and great in this town, and supported by sons and brothers. Now be the first to come and do what the king commands, as all the Gentiles and the people of Judah and those that are left in Jerusalem have done. Then you and your sons will be numbered among the Friends of the king, and you and your sons will be honored with silver and gold and many gifts." (1 Maccabees 1:17-18)

Similar to Satan's proposition with Yeshua, the Greek officials attempted to bribe Mattathias with physical wealth in exchange for worship and sacrifices to their gods. Mattathias declined saying:

"Even if all the nations that live under the rule of the king obey him, and have chosen to obey his commandments, every one of them abandoning the religion of their ancestors, I and my sons and my brothers will continue to live by the covenant of our ancestors. Far be it from us to desert the law and the ordinances. We will not obey the king's words by turning aside from our religion to the right hand or to the left." (1 Maccabeus 1:20-22)

After Mattathias vowed to continue walking in the righteous path of YHWH, others chose to worship the gods of the king, and Judas became filled with holy rage, and slew them; along with the king's officials who brought the proposition to worship their gods.

Afterwards, he appointed his son as leader of arms, and became even more offensive in his approach. He formed an army; some to defend and some to plunder new territories for YHWH. He forcibly circumcised the uncircumcised among the Jews, he hunted down the arrogant and their work, and he never allowed the sinner to have the upper hand.

What To Do When Authority Changes Hands

When a territory is plundered, the first thing the victorious military must do is to make known that new supervision is in town. Similarly, when an operating business changes ownership, the new owner must analyze the operations of the business and make changes in order to ensure his success with his new purchase. Branding usually changes, financial management changes, new rules are set in place, and new leadership is appointed.

Exodus 34:13:

You shall tear down their **altars**, break their pillars, and cut down their sacred poles

Deuteronomy 7:5:

But this is how you must deal with them: break down their **altars**, smash their pillars, hew down their sacred poles, and burn their idols with fire.

Your Territory: Your Body, Soul, and Mind

When you have changed your allegiance from the kingdom of darkness to the Kingdom of Light, you must undergo a similar process of looking over your operations, your rules, your ways, and be submissive to your new leadership. You have to tear down the altars you previously praised and reorder your ways. This process takes analyzing, meditation on the Word of YHWH, and prayer. Things like music, entertainment, leisure activities, connections, and environment will need to be analyzed. You must tear down the altar of mediocrity, tolerance, and compliance with the kingdom in darkness agenda, and replace that with a blatant and bold altar for the Most High God. If anything enters your gates whose purpose is not to enhance your ability to submit to the laws of YHWH, you MUST remove the altar. Every altar in every category of your life must be built on loving YHWH and loving others. As you read the Word of YHWH, you will identify ways that are unlike Yeshua, and you will need to repent and change them.

Tearing Down The Altars To Your Flesh

Your flesh demands attention. In my book *Someone Covets You*, I talked about the character of Pride and other fruits of the flesh. She is loud and always wants to be heard. She demands expense regardless of the cost to others. She begs for others to praise her and all of her works, and if she does not get it, she complains and throws a tantrum. All of the works of the flesh operate similarly;

they demand leadership, and must be crucified into submission to YHWH. They attempt to control your thoughts, your will, and your ways with what "I want" or exaggerated needs. To tear down the altars to self, you have to sacrifice: Give when giving is hard, when you feel like withholding what you have because of what you want or you think that you need, you MUST give to break the clenches of the flesh.

Fast. What you feed will grow and what you deny food will die. If you cut off the source of food to your flesh (poor music choices, poor movie choice, poor relationship choices, poor book choices, poor eating habits, etc.) as a routine, you can regain the reigns that control the flesh, and render them over to the Spirit. The flesh cringes and bows in submission to the Spirit in the midst of a devoted fasting campaign. Fasting done regularly maintains that order of the flesh in submission to the Spirit.

Pray beyond your own desires. Sometimes the initial step to go into prayer can be the largest battle. Once you get into prayer and you are visiting Heavenly places, the battle is removed, but entry into the prayer world is where attacks of the enemy and the flesh are intense at times. Sometimes, you may see someone who needs prayer while you are in a "rush" to do something you really want to do; this is when you pray past your immediate desires.

Worship when it hurts. When we perceive that we are not getting our way, sometimes, we deny YHWH the worship He is due. In Job, we see he lost his children, the support of his wife and friends, his health, and a lot of his property in a time of testing. When we are being refined, it hurts. When impurities are being burned away, so that we can press into greater depths of the knowledge of YHWH, it does not always feel pleasant. Sing to YHWH the cry of that moment. Open your mouth and let the words flow to him in the instantaneous melody of the time. Lift your hands and dance to Him with the movement that expresses your concern. Pick up a pen and write or draw to Him from the expressions of your soul. He will come to your rescue; maybe not by redirecting you from the refining process, but by rendering you the grace to push past it.

The biggest lie under the sun is there is a place where laziness is okay, no work is welcomed, and reward stems from it. There is a price to be paid for everything including your present power and your eternal victory. The price is paid in the crucifixion of your flesh. Pressing in when your flesh is acting as dead weight speaking the most invoking pleasantries in your ear. "You know you want...", "You know how you should be treated", "Since they did this, you should do..."; these are all comments that can mislead you to followership of the flesh.

Plundering Territory Thru Evangelism

As your glory increases and the glorious presence of YHWH goes forth with you as a cloud, you will invade territories that rightfully belong to the kingdom of YHWH, but have been unlawfully stolen. People that have succumbed to enemy lies, property that is being misused for the exaltation of the enemy, and places that have an eerie feeling which signals you of enemy presences. To tear down the altars, you will have to follow the example of Yeshua.

Declare unlawful transactions as you see them. Send the enemy to flight. Command time to acknowledge the eternal reality of healing on those around you, declare blind eyes open, deaf ears hear, and the lame to walk. Take back the souls that the enemy has stolen. Take back the health that the enemy has stolen. Take back the property that the enemy is misusing. Redirect hearts to the Kingdom of Heaven. Declare judgment on the enemy as you send him in flight!

Physical Territories

Alot of the materials of YHWH are being misused to lead men into destruction. In the book of Enoch 8:1-9, it tells us how the fallen angels led men astray. It says:

Azazyel taught men to make swords, knives, shields, breastplates, the fabrication of mirrors, and the workmanship of bracelets and ornaments, the use of paint, the beautifying of the eyebrows, the use of stones of every valuable and select kind, and of all sorts of dyes, so that the world became altered. Impiety increased; fornication multiplied; and they transgressed and corrupted all their ways. Semjaza taught all the sorcerers, and dividers of roots: Armaros taught the solution of sorcery; Baraqijal taught the observers of the stars; Kokabel taught signs; Ezeqeel taught astronomy; And Asaqiel taught the motion of the moon. And men, being destroyed, cried out; and their voice reached to heaven."

In our times, the deeds taught by the fallen angels have increased. Yeshua forewarned us the end times would be comparable to Noah's time. Most people do not talk about how supernatural the evil was at the time of Noah. The fallen angels took an oath to marry women to multiply themselves on the Earth. As a result of the union, supernatural giants (up to 45 feet tall according to the book of Enoch) were born to women, and mankind did not have a solution for their care. They could not satisfy the appetites of the children and the nephilim ate their parents and others as a result. As a result of the unholy matrimony of angels and mankind, evil multiplied on the Earth to the extent that all of men's thoughts were evil, and YHWH chose to cleanse them from the Earth. Their ways are still present on the Earth and apparent thru sickness, fornication, hatred, bestiality, the drinking of blood, killing of men, abortion and prevention of multiplication among other deeds.

In our modern days, we see genetic tampering commonly. In Noah's time, the fallen angels were manipulating the seed of man to prevent the birth of the Promised Child, Yeshua, and the redemption of mankind. Today, occultists are summoning spirits, physically manifesting them calling them "aliens", gaining insight common to the insight in Noah's time. They are genetically modifying food, injecting diseases thru shots, changing genders, and even attempting to create "cloned" people: a counterfeit of the image of YHWH as seen in us. They want to clock you out and take you to their house early! They have been judged by YHWH. Their eternal plot is in pit of utmost torment for eternity and their hateful response to the decree is to bring as many people with them as they can. A lot of insight is being given as occultists summon the fallen angels to gain ancient insight to pollute the gene pool of the oblivious. Their tactics are all old, repeated throughout the Bible, and limited in power and authority, therefore, you should be plundering them, and bringing them into submission left and right!

The awesome news is that as the Ambassador of the Earth's world power, the universe's world power, and all creations' world power, you have been given the authority to take back unlawfully accessed territory to include people, places, and things. When you spot enemy tampering - AND - you have strong defense in place (very important because if you don't, you will be thrown around), then you can get into offensive strategies for entering enemy gates, and plundering the enemy. Offensive strategies include:

Plundering The Enemy Thru Intercession

Prayer, worship, and fasting to plunder enemy settlements in your friends, family, workplaces, city, state, nation, and world. Pray to redirect the hearts of your leaders to YHWH. Others are praying to lead them astray, so you MUST be prayerful to counteract the evil forces against your leaders! Once your body, soul, spirit, and property is brought under submission, you can intercede for others who have been taken captive by enemy forces. Battle in the Spirit on their behalf. Assign angels to keep watch over them. Encourage them and start to surround the enemy camp until he is smothered, and sent to flight.

Going in enemy gates

Overwhelm the gates the enemy has stolen by creating an atmosphere of praise, prayer, and worship. Feed them with good spiritual fruit, so that their spirits are restored to life, and they can reason against the enemies controlling tactics. Teach people how to prosper in relationships with their families, friends, and those around them. Teach them how to steward the gifts of YHWH well, and remove the enemy property (lies, deceit, hatred, etc.) he has imported into their hearts to keep them bound.

Going before the Courts of YHWH

Take others before the courts of YHWH in repentance to restore to them their rightful inheritance.

Staying in the presence of YHWH

In the presence of YHWH, He will speak, advise, and send allies to your aid. Do not attempt to plunder the enemy in optimism! You MUST plunder the enemy with faith. Remember: Faith is the substance that brings a spiritual reality into the physical realm.

Assigning angels

The angels can tickle ears, tap shoulders, fight battles, send insight, and help in other ways to expand the kingdom of YHWH. They are excited to hear assignments where they are assisting as you explore and advance the Kingdom of YHWH. Let YHWH know when you need back-up.

Doing intelligence

Previously, we spoke about how powerful military forces are always mindful of the strategies, tools, and ways of their enemy, so they can be well prepared in defense, and find weaknesses to exploit with their offense. You must be doing intelligence on yourself and your environment, and creating strategies to win.

Evicting the enemy from your family, neighborhood, city, and country

With your intelligence, you can be mindful of the enemy presence and create plans to evict their kingdom from your neighborhood, city, and country. For each level of authority, you MUST get authorization from the throne of YHWH. Do not simply attempt to bust into government roles and send the enemy fleeing without YHWH's authorization. You can intercede for them, but do not physically enthrone yourself without direct authorization.

Living Righteously

Living righteously creates an example; it is your glory. With righteous living, your glory becomes more blatantly apparent, and others are changed simply by the presentation of your righteousness.

Growing Spiritually

Desire time with YHWH and an understanding of His ways like the air that you breathe. If your absent from air without intention for even one minute, your body goes into a panic. Even though you may not stay consciously aware, YHWH is the gracious fabric that keeps all of the molecules of your presence in contact. It was His voice that caused everything to form, and the vibration of His voice is the fabric that holds everything we see together. Furthermore, YHWH is the beginning of every new thing you need and desire. He is the beginning of your desired opportunity, your desired relationship, and your desired environment, and your desired property. Without Him, your innermost desires (the ones you know and the ones that are so deeply seated that you may not be aware of them without intense meditation and submission of your thoughts) cannot be met.

Use your authority over nature

Natural laws were not intended to reign over us, but rather, we are supposed to have dominion over nature. The stars, the moon, the winds, the thunders, the lightning, the rain, the animals, the plants, and everything else that is a creation of YHWH on the Earth is what you have been given to rule over. You must learn how to operate your authority, so you can exercise the power.

CHAPTER EIGHT

WALK WITH YHWH, NOT BEHIND HIM!

The Story of Karen and Witchcraft

Karen was a witch for 10 years. She practiced many different occult things since she was 11 years of age. Her father was a Voodoo priest who worked alongside a principality to reign over a large territory in the northern states of the US.

She was the seventh child, and her parents dedicated her life to advancing the kingdom of their spiritual allegiance. At age 5, she began using cocaine that was laying around the house, and at age 10, her father began training her to govern a territory in the Southern States with Voodoo practices. Between drugs and voodoo, her decision-making was always altered by spiritual realities, but she kept her practices behind closed doors.

In her training, she learned how to teleport, so she did not have to use airplanes for flight, she learned how to stay rich by creating curses that would cause her customers to come back recurrently. She learned how to rid her territory of businesses or residents that would not advance the kingdom, and she learned how to train others to take territories with voodoo. Her training lasted more than one year and over the course of time, she learned many more things that classified her as "spiritually mature" and capable of governing a territory.

After one year of training, her father sent her away and instructed her to find a church and begin her mission. She began attending a church regularly; offering what she called, "holistic medicines" to the members. She called herself a "Christian", and those who learned her practices also called themselves "Christians". She created organizations for grief, the single, the fatherless, those struggling with health ailments, and others in distress. She would host different pampering gatherings at her house where she would do hair, nails, and skin care. When the dead skin would shed, when hair would shed, or nails would be clipped, she would keep the residue for casting spells. Her customers would feel they "need" her goods and services because of the heaviness of the spells on them. Eventually, the majority of the church members (to include the pastor) were recurring customers.

In addition to being very well known and highly depended upon in her region of residence, she traveled often. She explored the world thru teleportation; visiting numerous countries without the use of physical modes of transportation. When she would travel, she exemplified many powers: astro-projection, the ability to send demonic forces in response to her requests, and conversations with spiritual beings.

She received insight about the future because she had been a studying and practicing psychic for ten years. She called her future insight, "Prophesy", and many Christian people came to her for insight and advice. In church circles, she was called, "Prophetess". Karen became a very prominent Christian leader when she became terminally ill.

She attempted to handle her sickness with her potions, but to no avail. She burned incense and prayed, but her sickness seemed to bear a heavier and heavier weight. Karen became bedridden as a patient in the hospital, and was told she had only one month to live. Her followers became skeptical saying, "How can she be making potions that do not work for her?"

She lost many customers. She became very depressed and hopeless when a stranger walked into her hospital room. He glowed with joy and told her that he knew how she could be healed. Desperately, she said, "How?" He told her, "You must die to yourself, your current ways, and repent." He continued saying, "You have led thousands of people into witchcraft calling it 'Christianity'. Rather than teaching people how to be free, you enslave them, and the One True YHWH says this needs to stop. Are you willing?" She said, "Yes!", and followed the man in prayer; committing to abandon witchcraft. She was miraculously healed. She closed her business, began sharing the true gospel, and many were saved in the remainder of her lifetime.

A Price Has Been Paid For You

It does not matter how evil the deeds you have done may be, there is still a way out for you. The price has been paid for your freedom. YHWH, the Creator of Heaven and Earth wants to be able to sit face to face with you, tell you His plans, and enjoy eternal life creating and discovering unendingly. He has places He would like to show you and prosperous plans He would like to reveal to you. Are you open?

The big heart of YHWH would not let go of you even though

Adam had to be sent out of the place where His presence and abundance reaches the earth, the heart longing of YHWH for you is for fellowship. YHWH created you to fellowship with Him, and this desire could not be filled by any other being.

Get Intimate With YHWH!

YHWH wants you to see, feel, hear, and smell Him. We wants to walk alongside you as He did with Adam and Eve. Genesis 3:8 says, "Then the man and his wife heard the sound of the YHWH as he was walking in the garden in the cool of the day, and they hid from the YHWH among the trees of the garden." He wants to share dominion with you over the laws that confine the kingdom in darkness, and allow you to see Him as He is creating. He has granted you access to bring eternity into your present by faith. Apostle Renny Mclean described faith saying, "Faith is not blind. Faith is a compilation of what is said in Hebrews 11:4 backwards. Things seen in the spiritual realm as evidence+hope+confidence=Faith. When faith has been created by the compilation of things, evidence, hope, and confidence, then you can materialize the thing (healing, miracle, breakthrough, or blessing) now." For this reason, Yeshua was able to command time to reflect eternity saying, "Take your mat and walk!", or "Your sins are forgiven!".

There is a difference in walking behind someone and walking alongside someone. When you walk with someone, you see what direction they are currently going, and you are going WITH them. Many people submit to the curse placed on Adam, the wedge that was placed between him and YHWH; when communion was broken, and He began walking behind YHWH (in His past). Guess what? Time is like a cage that binds only the kingdom in darkness and those who are submitted to it. It binds the record of sin, and does not allow their reach into the realm of eternity. Even more, it is declining, decreasing, depleting, and will not return. When Galatians 3:36-38 says that we are "in Yahshua", it is telling us we are no longer behind or ensnared in the same cage as darkness, we are not subject to the location where time confines. The scripture says, "For as many of you as were baptized into Yahshua have put on Yahshua. There is neither Jew nor Greek, there is neither slave nor free, there is neither male nor female; for you are all one in the Messiah Yeshua." When you align with YHWH, you are a miracle magnet because you are outside of the cage of time in eternity. With the payment Yeshua made, you have faith access to Heaven, Eden, and all other territories YHWH has created for man to explore.

Many people make eternity much more difficult to comprehend because they comprehend it as a time zone rather than a location. Eternity does not mean, "Forever". It is a location outside of Earth's laws, and you can tap into it now by seeking Yeshua.

Get Access To Your Spiritual Senses So That You Can Identify Eternity

Eternity is a spiritual place that is recognized by the portions of your mind that are presently not in use. Science has re-affirmed the fact that the majority of the brain is not used. Only 10% of the brain function has been confirmed. Some scientists say the functions of the other 90% of the brain are simply unknown while scientists such as Albert Einstein say that the 90% is not in use. When our brains are connected to the spiritual realm, we are able to make use of the unused portions of our brain by using our spiritual sight, touch, hearing, and smell. Paul spoke about how we need to exercise our brains and restore the use of every part of our brains. In Hebrews 5:14, he said, "But solid food belongs to those who are of full age, that is, those who by reason of use have their senses exercised to discern both good and evil." You MUST exercise your spiritual senses! Step beyond the realm of hearing a message from a church, a pastor, or even your Bible, and jump into the realm where you can see the angels, the enemy, our Father, Yeshua, and you can identify the Holy Spirit. The Word became flesh, so you are being introduced to YHWH thru His love letter (the Bible), but now it's time you see Him and gain an intimate relationship with Him.

Here are some ways YHWH speaks to you:

- Audible voice (more in the Old Testament than in the new). He came upon (Old Testament) rather than indwelled (New Testament)

- inward (walk intimacy

- thoughts

- visions

- dreams

- angels

- gifts of the Spirit

- circumstances

- the Word of YHWH is the voice of YHWH

- People

- nature
  sharks came closer to the edges of the sea before 9/11

- instructions

- numerology (not so much about numbers but sequence) thru numerology, there is a patent of numbers, you will see an event and a name

When YHWH Speaks…

In dreams. Do you suppose how many believers joke with their dreams? For me, my dreams are my spiritual monitor; I know where I am with YHWH through my dreams, I know the position of the enemies as they assail against me through my dreams, I know what YHWH would have me do through my dreams. He talks to me that way. Sometimes, I see events before they come to pass through my dreams. Give attention to your dreams; YHWH talks to us through them.

His audible voice. Next to dreaming is the audible voice of YHWH. Some people do not believe YHWH does speak audibly to His children today. YHWH does speak aloud. He is a person and He speaks still audibly today.

Prophesy. YHWH does speak to us through prophecy today or even through prophets. To prophesy is to speak forth the divine council of YHWH, by way of foretelling-telling of things to come or forth-telling-speaking forth the purpose of YHWH for today. It is important we pay attention to prophecy. Despise not prophesying, the book says. (1 Thess.5:20)

Spirit to Spirit. Again, YHWH through His Holy Spirit speaks to us. His Spirit communicates with our spirits. We are spirit beings so we are capable of having the Spirit of YHWH speak to our spirits in so many ways: the inner witness, deep impressions, peace as an empire etc. YHWH does speak to us through His Spirit.

As a message from the angels. Angels are YHWH's special messengers sent forth to minister and wait on believers who are heirs of salvation. They bring YHWH's message to us every now and then. YHWH speaks to us through them today.

Rather than battling in the dark; unaware or inattentive of your enemies or your allies, be on the offense; listening to YHWH in your dreams, visions, trances, or other avenues of communication! The Bible says if you ask for an answer and seek Him for it, you will knock, and the door will be opened for you. Ask your Father and He will answer you regarding your current concerns. Be ready for His response thru whichever portal He communicates.

In his book, *Seeing in the Spirit*, the Praying Medic describes how spirits and physical bodies differ in the way that communication is transmitted. In the physical, our communication is transmitted thru breath going thru the vocal chords which creates a wave of vibration that is transmitted to the other person's ear canal and interpreted in the brain. In the communication between spiritual beings, the physical structures are typically not used. Rather, your hearing and your speech is typically performed by your heart, and your seeing is performed in the display of your mind thru thought impressions. The thoughts you cannot manipulate are those that are received by another source; either from the kingdom in darkness or from the Kingdom of Light.

How You Can Identify Your Flesh

Your flesh can be identified by its selfish intent; typically making "I" statements that uplift self like, "I am too good for that", "How will this benefit me", "I want", "I like" and statements like that. Words that describe flesh statements are all those that begin with self, "Self-love", "self-reliant", "Self-sufficient", "Self-esteem", and so on. In order to be led by the Spirit, you must crucify your flesh. Rather than being ego or flesh controlled, you allow your choices, your will, and your expressions to be based on what you see or hear from the Kingdom of Light.

How To Identify The Voices Of Darkness

The kingdom of darkness desires to steal, kill, or destroy from your assignment. They leave thought impressions that cause destruction to your assignment or the assignment of those that you are connected to. They are professional tempters, and they have done surveillance to recognize the weaknesses in your lineage. They have records they can track that go back to Adam and Eve, and these records can easily be traced in your DNA. Their voices will take peace, joy, love, unity, faith, hope, and other virtues that are vital for your wellbeing. If you are not discerning or you are not keeping a record of the virtues the Father has given you, they will steal from you, and you will not even identify it.

How To Identify The Voices Of Light

The Kingdom of Light desires to increase, restore, and advance your assignment. Their voices add nutrients to your Spirit, promote you, increase your abilities, and give you life. The angels are happy to transmit words to increase you. YHWH loves you affectionately and He loves to deposit increase into your spirit. They abundantly pour revelation in your Spirit and you can identify the deposits of the Kingdom of Light when your un-manipulated ideas increase you in your function to the Kingdom.

The Merge Of The Spirit with the Physical

Regarding the spiritual senses of touch and smell, they are typically mistaken with the physical senses although they are perceived thru the spiritual senses. For example, you may smell smoke, but you cannot find a physical source or you may feel someone tapping you, and when you look around, you cannot find anyone there.

My husband described a time when he was driving after a long day of work, and he fell asleep on the highway. He completely drove off of the highway onto the access road parallel to it. When he got onto the access road, he felt taps on his shoulder, and he jumped up, but noticed no one. Then, he smelled very strong perfume, and he knew that an angel had been sent to wake him up, and help him get home safely. Thanks to YHWH!

Blot Out Transgression From Your DNA

The midst of all the joys, love and fellowship with Father: Adam and Eve gave into the devil's lie, distrusting YHWH's word and the result: they lost their right of rule to their territory. They forfeited their fellowship and love playing with YHWH almighty, His law has been violated, He must be just to Himself, to Satan who brought about the fall and to Adam too: He chased them out of their inheritance and place of fellowship and son-ship was lost. But thank YHWH for the marvels of His grace: YHWH, the all-knowing had a plan.

In her books, *Trading Floors*, Judy Coventry described how Sin has intellectual property she licenses freely in exchange for a wage. Liens are placed on our blessings and records are kept in our DNA to account for the use of their intellectual property. The University of Utah describes these basic principles regarding the markings in our DNA. They say:

- Each spot on a microarray contains multiple identical strands of DNA.

- The DNA sequence on each spot is unique.

- Each spot represents one gene.

- Thousands of spots are arrayed in orderly rows and columns on a solid surface (usually glass).

- The precise location and sequence of each spot is recorded in a computer database.

The way the kingdom in darkness intends for you to pay back these debts documented in your DNA is by debts rationed in the genes or "gene rations", otherwise known as generational curses. The good news is all of these debts can be cancelled in court, and even better, we can take on the DNA of YHWH. Did you hear me? We can take on the DNA of YHWH!

In his book, *The Realms of the Kingdom Volume 1*, Ian Clayton explains the transformation of your DNA. You can change your DNA to the DNA of YHWH thru communion. Spiritually, you take in the blood and body of Yeshua in communion, and declare access to YHWH of every part of your body (spiritually and physically). As this prophetic act physically goes through your blood in digestion, YHWH spiritually blots out the marks, spots, and stains the enemy has rationed in your DNA record. He sets you FREE!

The Covenant of The Blood

Saddled with the responsibility of keeping, tending, to watch and to rule over all of YHWH's creation as far as the earth was concerned, but with just a little test for assurance of loyalty; Adam and Eve turned the earth over to Satan, YHWH's enemy the moment they accepted Satan's deal and questioned YHWH's integrity.

In the garden, the serpent sold his idea to Adam and Eve. When he bought it and gave in to the lies of the enemy in the place of the word of YHWH, the singular action legally surrendered Adam's ownership to the serpent.

Adam legally gave away the earth as his place of domain to the devil and sold all of his unborn generation (you and I) to the enemy of YHWH. In ignorance, we also trade our blessings for quick unsatisfying access to Sin's intellectual property. Lies, idolatry, adultery, sexual immorality, and other sins are technology patented and secured by the kingdom in darkness. They know when you use their property and they place liens on your blessings. YHWH is the Law Giver, His word is law, His dealings with all of His creation are based on legal ground; He is just and cannot violate His orders. Satan on the other hand, understands the law and knows how to use it against humans; he did and he succeeded at his first attempt: that was how you and I got ourselves in the mess that we are in today. (See Deut. 32:3-4 and Romans 5:12-21)

When YHWH created Adam, He gave him breath, and he became a live being. Most people are aware of the ability of the lungs to transport oxygen, but unaware that the blood is the major transporter of the life, nutrients, living water, and breath that enables the body to live. The blood is the part of the body that transports the breath of life given by YHWH to man.

Blood is life. It is the means of transport for your soul. Blood keeps the soul in the body as it flows throughout. Leviticus 17:11 says, For the life of the flesh is in the blood, and I have given it to you on the altar to make atonement for your souls; for it is the blood that makes atonement, by reason of the life [which it represents]."

The blood is also a tool of accounting. The blood is able to transport cleansing or filth. Genesis 4:22 says, "Reuben answered them, "Did I not tell you, 'Do not sin against the boy'; and you would not listen? Now the accounting for his blood is required [of us for we are guilty of his death]." Curses and blessings are attached to the blood. Inheritance or debt is transmitted in the blood, and as I said previously, spiritual debts are tracked in the DNA markings in the blood.

The only way for blood to be cleansed is thru the process of transfusion whereby your blood is exchanged for the blood of another. Then, you take on the DNA advantages and disadvantages written in the other person's blood. The Bible tells us that blood speaks even after the spirit has departed; it can disclose guilt or innocence. Genesis 4:10 says, "The Lord said, "What have you done? The voice of your brother's [innocent] blood is crying out to Me from the ground [for justice]." Blood can tell of iniquity or peace, transgression or righteousness, and the blood cries as a witness even after the spirit has departed.

When anything touches blood, it takes on the blessings or curses associated with it. For this reason, when Cain attempted to cover his shame and guilt after killing his brother, he was cursed from the ground where his brother was buried. YHWH instructed us not to eat blood, not to shed blood with our hands, not to have intercourse while blood is being released, and in the instance we come in contact with blood, He tells us that we have to be set apart for a period of uncleanliness. Blood is sacred because it is the main ingredient that transmits the breath of YHWH thru man in the physical realm.

Witches, warlocks, and other occultists like Karen know that unless they have blood, they do not have power. Satan understands how sacred human blood is. He understands blood contains a holiness because it transports the holy breath of the Almighty God even despite our fallen nature.

This fact transcended from the fall of man. Since man fell and YHWH slaughtered a lamb to clothe him, covering his shame, man has required blood to commune with YHWH. Because there were only two human beings at that time (both fallen), the blood of the animals was the most pure form of blood that was available. YHWH maintained the covenant of redemption thru animal blood until the time of Yeshua. The blood of the animals was never enough to cleanse the DNA record of man because the animal is not created in the likeness of YHWH, and therefore, they do not carry the breath that YHWH breathed into Adam.

Still, to this day, many do not know of the redemption they can receive thru the blood of Yeshua the Messiah. When he died the brutal death on the cross, his blood was shed for you. With his blood in communion, a spiritual blood transfusion takes place. As you drink the blood (symbolized prophetically by wine or grape juice) and eat the flesh (symbolized prophetically by bread), you are blotting out all iniquity that cries in your blood, all guilt is being erased, and all righteousness and inheritance from his blood is replacing all of the debt in yours.

You may have accessed beautiful spiritual places, had lots of fun teleporting across the world, gaining riches, gaining insight about the future, and even visiting beautiful heavenly places in the spiritual realm, but there is more you cannot access without the blood of Yeshua. Where every other god and power source falls short, is complete through the blood of Yeshua the Messiah. Any healing, sickness, heartache, or failure can be erased in Yeshua' name. No other name has the same power. This is not simply my opinion. In every generation, the kingdom in darkness has attempted to silence the voices that speak out about the blood to no avail. Persecution until death, government laws, religious hatred, and the most severe opposition has attempted to silence witnesses of the power of YHWH, and guess what? The power of the blood has only grown a wider audience with more testimonies and evidences of healing and deliverance from every form of opposition known to man. Missing body parts have grown, the blind have been given sight, the deaf have been given their hearing, the cripple has been given the ability to walk, and the dead have been resurrected in every continent as a result of the power of the blood.

Choose this day whom you will serve. Choose this day whether you will try to swim your way out of sin and heartache by your own physical deeds, by paying the price of another god, or by receiving the inheritance that is freely granted to you by opening your mouth and confessing that Yeshua the Messiah is your Lord.

The Father undertook a great sacrifice for you. No other god has willingly sacrificed their firstborn son out of love in exchange for fellowship with you. The God of Abraham, Isaac, and Jacob willingly sacrificed His only son, lost communion with Him, sent Him to bear the worst torture of Earth in a brutal crucifixion. He died and experienced even greater torture in hell where the weight of sorrow, fear, despair, and pain for man exceeds even the most abusive and painful tyranny of the Earth. In Hell, Yeshua visited the region of Abraham's bosom where righteous souls had been in Sheol and the region of torment where wicked souls were tormented. He took the keys that bore the authority of Satan to deceive and trap people in eternal damnation. With the keys in hand, he announced the end to Sin's authority over man, and he resurrected from hell and the grave with the power in his hands; bringing with him all those that believed. He walked on the Earth for 40 days alongside many others that rose from death with him. After 40 days, he ascended to Heaven leaving us the promise of power. Today, you have been given the keys of authority to Heaven and Earth. You have been authorized to subdue Sin and all those that work in the kingdom in darkness. People tormented in their minds, in their bodies, in their workplaces, and in our world, can be set free by your authority when you assume your position as joint heir with the Messiah.

The good news is all of these debts can be cancelled in court, and even better, we can take on the DNA of YHWH. Did you hear me? We can take on the DNA of YHWH! In his book, The Realms of the Kingdom Volume 1, Ian Clayton explains the transformation of your DNA.

You can change your DNA to the DNA of YHWH thru communion. Spiritually, you take in the blood and body of YHWH in communion, and declare access to YHWH of every part of your body (spiritually and physically). As this prophetic act physically goes thru your blood in digestion, YHWH spiritually blots out the marks, spots, and stains that the enemy has rationed in your DNA record. He sets you FREE!

You must submit to the hierarchy of Heaven and you can be endued with access to the most royal parts of creation in the spiritual places. When you are submitted, you will be entrusted with a godly inheritance and power as a joint heir with Yeshua the Messiah.

The Covenant of Adoption

In adoption, the person in government custody has a record of all that happened in their life: their abuse, their punishments, the wrong deeds, their schools, their foster homes, their medical record, and much more. This record must be reviewed by adopting parents prior to the adoption. When the parents agree they are willing to adopt the child knowing everything about their past, they must sign several documents and stand before a court confessing their willingness and capability to raise the child. Specifically in the Roman adoption process, after a king would adopt a child, they would sign, and have seven witnesses sign on the adoption paperwork stating they are willing to assist in training the child prior to their training with the king. Once the king and the seven witnesses had signed, the record of the child was blotted clean, and a new life was begun.

Similar to the adoption process for a child in governmental custody, the fall of man forfeited your residence in the presence of YHWH, and created a record. Sin assumed authority of you and all that was granted to you by YHWH. The blood covenant of Yeshua restored you to righteousness. Ephesians 1:4-6 says, "For he chose us in him before the creation of the world to be holy and blameless in his sight. In love he predestined us for adoption to son-ship through Yeshua the Messiah, in accordance with his pleasure and will— to the praise of his glorious grace, which he has freely given us in the One he loves."

The book of Esther shows the story of a young orphan born in the Persian Empire. When controversy broke out between King Artaxerxes, and his wife, Queen Vashti, the king decided to evict the queen, and relieve her from her role. The king sought a new wife, and many women of the kingdom were chosen as potential brides for the king. Esther was one such candidate. Esther 2:9 says, "Now the young woman pleased Hegai and found favor with him. So he quickly provided her with beauty preparations and her [portion of] food, and he gave her seven choice maids from the king's palace; then he transferred her and her maids to the best place in the harem." The seven handmaidens were assigned to train her to maturity as the Queen of the Persian Empire. For one whole year, she had to be pampered and trained about how to be a queen in the Persian Empire before she was eligible to be elected by the king as the Queen.

The set apart assembly (the body of believers in Yahshua) are being prepared to be the bride of the Messiah. Just as Esther was given seven handmaidens to prepare her for the king, the Father has assigned the seven spirits of YHWH who sit in front of his throne to you. Isaiah 11:2 tells us who the seven spirits of YHWH are. It says, The Spirit of the Lord will rest on him— the Spirit of wisdom and of understanding, the Spirit of counsel and of might, the Spirit of knowledge and fear of the Lord—.

Many people are mistakenly saying that the seven spirits of YHWH are seven manifestations of the Holy Spirit, but John and Solomon amongst others show us the seven spirits were separate beings (angels) that were separate creations seated **BEFORE** the throne; submitted to the authority of the Father, Son, and Holy Spirit who are seated **ON** the throne. We know they are assigned to roam the Earth. Revelations 1:4 says, "John, to the seven churches that are in [the province of] Asia: Grace [be granted] to you and peace [inner calm and spiritual well-being], from Him Who is [existing forever] and Who was [continually existing in the past] and Who is to come, and from the seven Spirits that are before His throne,". The seven spirits of YHWH are residents of Heaven assigned to Earth as helpers to equip us to spiritual maturity. Ian Clayton says they equip us to govern the Kingdom of YHWH on Earth as it is in Heaven.

Galatians 4:1-2 says, "Now what I mean is as long as the inheritor (heir) is a child and under age, he does not differ from a slave, although he is the master of all the estate; But he is under guardians and administrators or trustees until the date fixed by his father." Similar to the child who is under guardians and administrators for an appointed time, the Father has given us the seven spirits to give us insight, so we can be good stewards of the inheritance we receive from YHWH. The seven spirits are a part of the covenants of YHWH: the rainbow symbolized with its seven colors, the creation symbolized by its seven days, and the return of the Messiah symbolized by the seven seals."

The spirit of the Lord will rest on him—

The spirit of the Lord is different than the spirit of the Sovereign Lord. In Isaiah 61:1, we see the distinction of the Spirit of the Sovereign Lord. Scripture says, "[The Year of the Lord's Favor] The Spirit of the Sovereign Lord is on me, because the Lord has anointed me to proclaim good news to the poor."

The spirit of Wisdom

In Proverbs 8:22-31, Wisdom describes her role in your spiritual maturity, She describes her sequence in the creation week, and her delight in the creations of YHWH. It says:

"The Lord brought me forth as the first of his works,

before his deeds of old;

I was formed long ages ago,

at the very beginning, when the world came to be.

When there were no watery depths, I was given birth,

when there were no springs overflowing with water;

before the mountains were settled in place,

before the hills, I was given birth,

before he made the world or its fields

or any of the dust of the earth.

I was there when he set the heavens in place,

when he marked out the horizon on the face of the deep,

when he established the clouds above

and fixed securely the fountains of the deep,

when he gave the sea its boundary

so the waters would not overstep his command,

and when he marked out the foundations of the earth.

Then I was constantly at his side.

I was filled with delight day after day,

rejoicing always in his presence,

rejoicing in his whole world

and delighting in mankind.

The spirit of Wisdom directs prosperous creativity. She desires to give mankind prosperity, but she desires relationship. Moses, Joshua, and Solomon are said to have been filled with the Holy Spirit.

The spirit of Understanding

The Spirit of Counsel

The spirit of Might

The Spirit of knowledge

The spirit of the fear of the Lord

On the contrary, we know that God (the Father, Son, and the Holy Spirit) are the beginning and the end; not a creation, but the Creators. Scriptures say:

I am the Alpha and the Omega, the First and the Last (the Before all and the End of all). (Revelations 22:13)

In the beginning [before all-time] was the Word (the Messiah), and the Word was with YHWH, and the Word was YHWH Himself. He was present originally with YHWH. All things were made and came into existence through Him; and without Him was not even one thing made that has come into being. In Him was Life, and the Life was the Light of men. (John 1:1-4)

You must give the covenant of adoption power in your life, be filled with the Holy Spirit, and learn from the seven spirits of YHWH how you can govern on Earth as it is in Heaven.

You can now go before the throne of YHWH and into the Holy of Holies!

Having raised Yeshua from the dead, the doorway into YHWH's presence is now open freely and eternally for whosoever will. No more limitation and selection as far as approach to YHWH is concerned. You can go now into YHWH's Holy presence-throne of grace and receive help for your every need upon the one and only sacrifice of the Messiah Yeshua. (See Hebrews 10:14)

The work Yeshua did covers all the need of man for time and for eternity; it interconnects all that is YHWH, whether it be the Holy Spirit, the Father Himself, His holy angels, etc., the sacrifice of the Messiah gave us access to all there is to YHWH. The new creation has the Holy Spirit at his disposal; the redeemed man has YHWH's holy angels working for him. These are rights and privileges we enjoy as ambassadors of the kingdom of YHWH. Are they not all ministering spirits sent forth to minister for those who shall be heirs of salvation? (See John 14:16 and Hebrews 1:14)

CHAPTER NINE

STORE TREASURE IN HEAVEN

Daniel made an investing transaction that yielded him a return beyond what compound interest could calculate. When the Jews were in exile in Babylon, Daniel earned his prestige by communion with YHWH. He imported wisdom from Heaven that led the kingdom beyond their current circumstances. His interpretation of dreams and advice of how to transcend the current turmoil gained him prestige, and others became jealous. They gained understanding about the key the ingredient that he required in order to continue to maintain his communion with YHWH, and therefore they attacked his prayer life. A law was placed that forbid the worship of gods other than the image of Nebuchadnezzar. In the face of turmoil, Daniel chose to forsake earthly favor to store his treasure up in Heaven. Daniel sacrificed his reputation, his time, his prestige, his food, and his life. With his earthly life on the line, Daniel began sowing prayer, intercession, commitment, and wisdom into the Kingdom of Heaven. In response, an angel came to him, and told him his balance. He said, "But you, go your way till the end; for you shall rest, and will arise to your inheritance at the end of the days."

Investing in Heaven vs. Investing on Earth

Investing is a crucial practice to create wealth. Yeshua tells you to store your treasure in Heaven rather than in Earth, but how do you store treasure in Heaven while you are on Earth?

Who doesn't want to be wealthy eternally? Well, the truth is that in order to do so, you must invest in Heaven. The most important investments are not in our physical view. If you have been investing mostly on Earth, you will find the interest rates typically do not exceed 20% (generously speaking), taxes take away from your profit, charges and other fees decrease your profit, and there is always a slight chance of robbery. Contrarily, in Heaven returns are exceeding 100%. Heaven is the most profitable place to invest!

Everyone on Earth will experience material economic collapse someday. Whether you like it or not money is temporal. Property is temporal. Everything that you see with your physical eye is temporal. Everything that you accumulate with your physical body is temporal, and the economic collapse of your physical wealth will arrive one day because you (like everyone else) will cross from the physical realm to the spiritual realm one day. When you die, you inevitably face the demise of your physical currency and all of your physical earnings. At this time, you will be faced with the reality that there is life beyond death. In the eternal life, you can be prosperous eternally or poor eternally, and you have two locations you can choose to reside (Heaven or Sheol), but the decision MUST be made before your last breath. The day where you cross into the spiritual realm may be in this lifetime (because thru spiritual practices, you can explore spiritual places), and it may be at death. You may live prosperous in this physical reality, but what does your reality look like beyond this physical zone? Are you aware of the currency of the spiritual realm? Have you decided where you will reside after you shake hands with death? Will he be transporting you to a place of joy or torment? Let's make some choices today, okay? Let's decide to be rich in paradise after death. In order to do so, let's first discuss how you can store up treasure in Heaven (the capitol of Eternity in paradise).

The treasures of the Earth are money, property, natural resources, precious stones, food, water, etc. Yeshua told you wealth on Earth has the ability to rot, be eaten by pests, or stolen by others, but in Heaven, your treasure does not wear, it does not wilt, and it is not "naturally" depreciating. He also told you if we have all of your treasure stored up on the Earth (in the physical realm), then your heart will be there also. One step further, we know that when your heart is consumed by love for your physical treasure, it becomes and idol, and then, you would be breaking the first of the Ten Commandments which says:

"Thou shalt have no other gods before me"

What is Eternity?

Eternity is a place you can go to today. Eternity is not a time zone. It does not mean forever because even that is a measurement of time. Eternity was created before time. Time is only a tiny speck in comparison to the vastness of Eternity. Time (as we know it) only effects Earth's inhabitants. Eternity is a place.

When Yeshua died and rose, his blood paid for your flight to Eternity, and his act of going into Sheol, and taking the keys of the enemy, gives him sole authority to remove you from eternal suffering, and invite you to Eternity in paradise: no pain, suffering, sickness, evil, or lack. In Eternity, Heaven is the capitol of a huge world that is beyond your ability to fully discover. The Father, Son, and Holy Spirit are present in Eternity and they are the most humble and approachable leaders of all time. They desire to have a relationship, sit down face to face, and chat with you one on one. They are always creating something new majestic and beyond human comprehension, so everything (the inhabitants, the plants, rivers, and skies) are always glorifying Him because of how awesome He is and how awesome everything He creates is. YHWH, the Father of all, His Son, and the Holy Spirit are Kings of Eternity. You can close your eyes, and ask YHWH to escort you into the realm of eternity, and because Yeshua paid for your flight, you can go. When you go to Eternity, you first must go beyond time into the realm of faith (read this as if I am giving you directions to a location because I am). Once you arrive, you will find that money, talents, or physical goods are not a sufficient means to trade for anything. Furthermore, your physical possessions are too dirty and adulterated to enter into Eternity. If you want to acquire things in the eternal realm, you MUST face the fact Yeshua put before you thousands of years ago when he said what is written in Matthew 6:19-21. He said:

"Do not store up for yourselves treasures on earth, where moth and rust consume and where thieves break in and steal; but store up for yourselves treasures in heaven, where neither moth nor rust consumes and where thieves do not break in and steal. For where your treasure is, there your heart will be also."

How To Refocus Your Attention To Invest in Heaven

When following what Yeshua said, you would know you need to change your focus in TWO ways:

1. Refocus your attention from accumulating things here on Earth where EVERYTHING will depreciate

2. Focus your attention on accumulating things in the eternal realm where EVERYTHING will accumulate

Similar to ancient style trading where my goods or services can be traded in exchange for your goods or services, we must implement the process of trading in order to accumulate wealth in Heaven. When you exercise your ability here on Earth, wealth is transferred into your accounts in Heaven. You're probably asking yourself, "What can I trade here on Earth to accumulate wealth in the treasuries in Heaven?" Let me tell you some…

Goods That Can Be Righteously Traded In Heaven

- Righteousness

Righteousness is goodness, virtuousness, morality, integrity, dignity, rectitude, honor, decency, respectability, nobility, worthiness, and purity. Righteousness is based on the Word of YHWH: the words spoken directly to you, thru others, and in the Bible. Exodus 19:5 says, "Now therefore, if you obey my voice and keep my covenant, you shall be my treasured possession out of all the peoples." With this, we know we become the treasure (equivalent to physical money) in Eternity. In exchange for our obedience to the voice of YHWH, you gain favor, and VIP positioning in Eternity. More righteousness = More favor. Proverbs 15:16 says, "In the house of the righteous there is much treasure, but trouble befalls the income of the wicked." The house that King Solomon spoke of in scripture was not only a physical structure, he was speaking of the house of the righteous as a spiritual structure as well.

Matthew 6:31-33 says:

"Therefore do not worry, saying, 'What will we eat?' or 'What will we drink?' or 'What will we wear?' For it is the Gentiles who strive for all these things; and indeed your heavenly Father knows you need all these things. But strive first for the kingdom of YHWH and his righteousness, and all these things will be given to you as well."

In Matthew 6:31-33, Yeshua is encouraging you to go to Eternity! Go to Heaven! When you get there, you will find ALL of the resources that you need to import into Earth to prosper: hope, perseverance, supernatural energy, healing, ideas, connections, opportunities, wisdom, etc.

- Wisdom

Wisdom is not an object; it is a spirit. When the spirit of wisdom teaches you, then you have instruction, which is also a holy treasure. When the treasure is given to you, you can share discerningly to advance the Kingdom of YHWH. The spirit of Wisdom teaches you how to walk in righteousness. Without her, it is impossible to comprehend how to live in a righteous manner. When you invite the spirit of wisdom into your presence, the commands and words she gives should be stored up because they are holy treasures; useful on Earth and in Heaven. In Proverbs 2:1-5, the spirit of Wisdom says, "My child, if you accept my words and treasure up my commandments within you, making your ear attentive to wisdom and inclining your heart to understanding; if you indeed cry out for insight, and raise your voice for understanding; if you seek it like silver, and search for it as for hidden treasures—then you will understand the fear of the Lord and find the knowledge of YHWH."

- Truth

Truth grants you liberty. Without truth, you will be in bondage, and even worse, you may be unaware you are in bondage. Lack, sickness, or simply just feeling "stuck" stems from lies planted in your soul by the kingdom in darkness. When you find the truth, you will find your liberty.

- Faith

Faith is not hope, trust, or optimism. Faith is a substance that can pull things from the eternal realm into your current time zone. In the realm of faith, you can see things in Eternity. When you see things in eternity, you gain the confidence, hope, and assurance that when compounded will enable you to pull the eternal reality into the physical reality now.

- Giving

Yeshua told us about a key law of eternal increase that begins by giving. He said, "Give, and it will be given to you. A good measure, pressed down, shaken together, running over, will be put into your lap; for the measure you give will be the measure you get back." (Luke 6:38) Many people give without the sight to see their increase, but a transfer of wealth takes place in Heaven with every pure-hearted gift. You can give of your property, ideas, solutions, prayers, prophetic utterances, compliments, connections, time, services, or money. Yeshua said, "Give to everyone who begs from you, and do not refuse anyone who wants to borrow from you." (Matthew 5:42) Though giving is a law of eternal increase, the Bible goes further to tell us to pay special attention to give to the poor, orphans, and widows. When we give a portion of our increase to support the work of YHWH (the tithe), give to the poor, orphans, and widows, different portals of blessing open up to us. One law of giving that is HIGHLY overlooked says, "Every third year you shall bring out the full tithe of your produce for that year, and store it within your towns; the Levites, because they have no allotment or inheritance with you, as well as, the resident aliens, the orphans, and the widows in your towns, may come and eat their fill so the Lord your God may bless you in all the work that you undertake." (Deuteronomy 14:28)

- Glory

Glory is a covering; a garment that communicates an impression to all those around you. Your glory can be seen in the way your adorned, but even more so in the words that you speak and the actions that submit to them. The book of Sirach 1:11 says, "The fear of the Lord is glory and exultation, and gladness and a crown of rejoicing." When we give glory to YHWH thru worship, praise, prayers, fasting, and crucifying our flesh, we adorn His garment, and in return our glory increases. Yeshua told us our glory can encourage others to glorify YHWH because they will see the transformation in us. He said, "In the same way, let your light shine before others, so they may see your good works and give glory to your Father in heaven." (Matthew 5:16) Although glory is good and it distinguishes us a royal heir of Eternity, the Fear of the Lord provides an even greater covering. "The fear of the Lord is like a garden of blessing, and covers a person better than any glory." (Sirach 1:11)

- The Fruits of the Spirit

In the physical realm, fruit is apples, pears, peaches, and so on. Physical fruit can be contaminated with pesticides, poor soil, and other bad gardening practices. When Yeshua said we can increase in Heaven in a way we do not experience depreciation, one such investment is in spiritual fruit. Spiritual fruit yields a very high return on investment on the Earth and in Heaven. On Earth, when you invest spiritual fruit in people, in return, you get opportunities, loyalty, prayer, monetary blessings, customers, improved relationships, and much much more. Additionally, your vats are filled with more fruit because you have sown from your supply into the accounts of someone else. Galatians 5:22-23 says, "the fruit of the Spirit is love, joy, peace, patience, kindness, generosity, faithfulness, gentleness, and self-control. There is no law against such things."

Contrarily, you can surrender your blessings by trading with the enemy. The kingdom in darkness has goods and services they are excited to share with you. They are lies, immorality, theft, and destruction. Yeshua said, "I tell you, on the day of judgment you will have to give an account for every careless word you utter;"(Matthew 12:36) Similar to a licensing agreement, when you use the goods created and owned by the kingdom in darkness, they license the goods out to you in exchange for your blessings (and when compiled), they take your life, and escort you to their eternal home: Sheol, the place of eternal suffering.

Exercise

1. Choose to welcome Yeshua as the King of your life. The prayer can be very simple or very profound. Your choice. You need to open your mouth and invite Yeshua into your presence. Say:

"Yeshua, I have heard of your works and your ways. I believe your death and resurrection is the solution to every problem I face in my life. I am placing you as King and Lord over my life, and I am pouring your blood over me from the top of my head to the sole of my feet. I understand you are my covering and the sole guardian of my heart, and I willingly give my heart to you. Just as the sacrifices of the Bible, I place myself as a living sacrifice unto you. Use my life to advance your Kingdom in Yeshua' name. Amen."

2. Invite the spirit of Wisdom from before the throne of YHWH into your presence to guide you in the paths of righteousness. Say:

"Father, I thank you that your word tells me you created the spirit of wisdom to instruct me to walk in the ways of righteousness. The blood of Yeshua paid for my access to the spirit of Wisdom. I welcome the spirit of Wisdom into my presence now".

2. Be conscious of the added insight you are receiving

3. Keep an inventory of the ideas, connections, prayers, giving, and other trade that is taking place: what's being added to you from Heaven and what you are investing into Heaven.

In an earlier chapter, we said YHWH's call comes with an inheritance and that inheritance is always territorial. YHWH gave Adam a garden, He gave Abraham the land of Canaan, He gave to David the stronghold of Zion and to Yeshua He gave the earth and the heaven; being a joint heir with the Messiah, we share in the inheritance the Father has given Yahshua. All authority in heaven and on earth has been given to Yeshua; we who believe in Him share in that all authority over the heaven and the earth. What belongs to Yeshua belongs to us; we are members of His body in particular, of His flesh and of His bones. (See Ephesians 5:30)

CHAPTER TEN

SURRENDER THE EYES OF YOUR MIND

For those who live according to the flesh set their minds on the things of the flesh, but those who live according to the Spirit set their minds on the things of the Spirit. To set the mind on the flesh is death, but to set the mind on the Spirit is life and peace.
-Romans 8:5-6

The Author's Investment Story

Two years ago, I bought an ATM as an investment. The goal was to place it in a location for a high return. Every time, I would go to the ATM to refill it or to perform maintenance, the most exciting part was to see the return I had received off of the initial investment that I made in the purchase. At times I would go to the ATM and it had been used a lot, and at times when I would go, it had not been used as much. Within the first year, it returned 100% of the initial investment, and that is without much store traffic.

How To Withdraw From Your Inheritance In The Kingdom Of Heaven

Similar to my investment story, the best part about investing is when you receive your balance with a substantial return, and when you can withdraw more than you put in. With Heaven, this is the case, you can withdraw more than you put in. You would probably ask, "Why would anybody give me back more than I put into the account?". I have asked the same question, and the answer is, "because of the mercy and grace of YHWH". The difference between the investment into the Kingdom of Heaven and the multiplied amount you can withdraw from the Kingdom of Heaven is called, grace and mercy. Our sins have placed a debt balance in our life, which Satan uses to place liens on your inheritance, but because YHWH takes your investment, and adds grace to it; justifying it by the blood of the Messiah, you're able to receive more than you invest. For this reason, Paul said:

Since all have sinned and fall short of the glory of YHWH; they are now justified by his grace as a gift, through the redemption that is in the Messiah Yeshua, whom YHWH put forward as a sacrifice of atonement by his blood, effective through faith. He did this to show his righteousness, because in his divine forbearance he had passed over the sins previously committed; (Romans 3:23-25)

Storing up treasure in Heaven is the most profitable investment you could ever make. Real Estate, stocks, bonds, liens, compounding interest, licensing agreements, intellectual property, or anything else cannot yield the returns that investing in Heaven can. They typically amass 20-25% generously speaking, whereas, your investment in Heaven will yield more than 100% returns eternally.

The problem for many people is after you have invested, how do you withdraw? The treasury of Heaven works differently than any other treasury or bank. They do not need your bank routing number, your mailing address, your social security number, or even your name; these things are pre-recorded (even the hair on your head). You do not need to fill out a withdrawal slip or drive to a certain location. Rather...

"To withdraw from the Kingdom, you must open spiritual gates, doors, and windows".

Occultists teach how you can open spiritual doors when they teach you about the "third eye", or the pineal gland. The pineal gland sits between the left and right hemispheres of the brain. One picture that is used to add imagery to the "third eye" on the back of the US one dollar bill. It is a pyramid with an eye in the center.

Science has proven on average, most people are only using 10% of their brains, while the other 90% remains dormant. The other 90% of the human brain has been dormant since the fall of Adam. When 100% of the human brain is in operation, you can see the spiritual realm and the physical realm; both as a mutual reality. Occultists teach by opening your third eye you tap into an increased level of intuition Demons, angels, spiritual pathways, doors, heavenly places, and demonic places can all be accessed when the entire brain is in use. In his article, How to Crack Open the Pineal Gland, Joshua Eagle said, " when dissected, the pineal gland actually contains photoreceptors just like our own two seeing eyes and is actually activated by light transmitted thru our two seeing eyes". Most people cannot handle both simultaneous realities without being overwhelmed because there is so much activity (good and bad) happening in each realm, however, people are being trained in occult practices that enable them to open the pineal gland.

Many people say:

- Why would YHWH keep the spiritual realm away from us?

- Why wouldn't He want us to operate in our authority?

- Why would He be keeping secrets from us?

- It seems YHWH is being greedy or He doesn't want us to know who we really are

YHWH Reveals As You Mature

Eve and Ezra had similar thoughts regarding why the people of YHWH do not have access to their inheritance. In the Bible, Ezra writes of the response to these questions about the human lack of power. He asked questions like, "Are other nations better than the one from which I descended?", and "Why do sinners seem to reap greater harvests?" YHWH sent an angel to respond to Ezra's questions. The Bible says:

Then the angel had been sent to me, whose name was Uriel, answered and said to me, "Your understanding has utterly failed regarding this world, and do you think you can comprehend the way of the Most High?" Then I said, "Yes, my lord." And he replied to me, "I have been sent to show you three ways, and to put before you three problems. If you can solve one of them for me, then I will show you the way you desire to see, and will teach you why the heart is evil." I said, "Speak, my lord." And he said to me, "Go, weigh for me the weight of fire, or measure for me a blast of wind, or call back for me the day that is past." I answered and said, "Who of those have been born can do that, that you should ask me about such things? "And he said to me, "If I had asked you, 'How many dwellings are in the heart of the sea, or how many streams are at the source of the deep, or how many streams are above the firmament, or which are the exits of Hades, or which are the entrances of paradise?' Perhaps you would have said to me, 'I never went down into the deep, nor as yet into Hades, neither did I ever ascend into heaven.' But now I have asked you only about fire and wind and the day—things that you have experienced and from which you cannot be separated, and you have given me no answer about them." He said to me, "You cannot understand the things with which you have grown up; how then can your mind comprehend the way of the Most High? And how can one who is already worn out by the corrupt world understand incorruption?" (2 Esdras 4:1-11 NRSV)

The Illegal Routes To The Spiritual Realm

Chants, focused meditation, lights, sex, intense vibration, certain music, certain movements of the body, the use of natural DMT and other hallucinogens at increased amounts to enter the spiritual realm (pharmakeia in Greek or sorcery), and drugs are all illegal ways the pineal gland can be open aside from direct communion with the Messiah.

Many people are teaching that when you open the pineal gland and meet other spirits the other spirits are your friends and you can reach a higher consciousness or place of ecstasy. The teaching that you will meet spirit guides, reach a higher state of consciousness, you will be like YHWH, or you will arrive at a place of ecstasy finds its origins in the Garden of Eden; same tactic and same lie packaged a little differently.

For a short period of time, you may find excitement tapping into the spiritual realm illegally, but if you play with fire, you will be burned. The "spirit guides" you may be channeling, the places of ecstasy, and the "higher states of consciousness you are reaching are all temporal illusions granted by fallen angels who themselves have received their verdict from Heaven stating they will be in Sheol experiencing eternal torment. They know they are bound to hell for life, so with the time they have left, they deceive in hopes to ruin the future plans of YHWH in you. Let me let you in on a secret…YHWH has the victory and the Earth will manifest very clearly very shortly. He created the fallen angels, and they chose to "be like YHWH" by rebelling against Him in hopes to win His praise. They can never be greater than their Creator. I suggest you get out of that tug of war, and choose the Creator over the creation; paradise over suffering. You're smart.

Yeshua told us the intent of the kingdom in darkness when he said, "Satan comes to steal, kill, and destroy". He arrives at his intended destination by taking you thru a series of miniscule lies until you are consumed like a pretzel in a web of falsehoods, then the next stop is death.

The Author's Experience With Illegal Spiritual Activity

I came the closest to death after multiple experiences where I had entered the spiritual realm unlawfully I personally was not a fan of drugs, secular meditation, yoga, or karate, but I did have unhealthy music choices, unhealthy movie choices, and unhealthy relationships. At one point, my environment had become very infiltrated with bad music I thought was normal, bad movies I did not personally watch (but those around me would, so they were in my house), and alcohol was in the house because I had a husband who would drink it. I was well aware my ex-husband heard voices in his mind that disabled him from making healthy choices, and I had voices, but I perceived them as my friend because they would help me to protect myself. At one point in time, the demons had completely taken possession of him, and were going to use him to kill me. We had not argued and we were not fighting. I was laying down and he was in another room. Suddenly, he came into the same room as I was in, and lifted me off the bed by my neck to the point that my feet dangled; unable to touch the ground. I began crying and shaping my lips for words to come out, but because my oxygen source was cut off, I could not speak. He looked at me nonchalantly in the face; disregarding my feelings and emotional outbreak. Within seconds of putting me down, he left the house, and I just cried. Many close attempts to take my life happened–all because I was positioning myself in an environment where demons could have free reign. It seemed normal. It seemed harmless. But, looking back, he and I had opened our lives, allowed demonic influences in, and would have supernatural shows of rage, hate, and discord when the atmosphere was fitting. The right atmosphere would increase our hormone balance, and enable us to hear the misleading voices clearly and loud.

The Legal Routes To The Spiritual Realm

The Bible references opening the eyes of the mind, spiritual gates, doors, and windows several times; there are legal and illegal routes of entry. In order to open spiritual gates, doors, and windows, legally, you must pay the price. You may be saying, "What price do I have to pay?" The price is not money, but the price is in relationship building with YHWH. Yeshua said, "I am THE way" and "I am the Door". What Yeshua was telling us is if we want to enter into the spiritual realm, He is the way and the door to it.

I pray the YHWH of our Lord Yeshua the Messiah, the Father of glory, may give you a spirit of wisdom and revelation as you come to know him, so that, with the eyes of your heart (opthalamos = the mind's eye) enlightened (fotisméni means illuminated), you may know what is the hope to which he has called you, what are the riches of his glorious inheritance among the saints, and what is the immeasurable greatness of his power for us who believes, according to the working of his great power. (Ephesians 1:17-19)

Great prophets of YHWH were able to receive great miracles from Heaven because they paid the price. The Bible tells us Yeshua is the beginning and the end, and throughout scripture, we see He interacted with the prophets of old even before His physical manifestation on the Earth. When they exercised the use of Yeshua as the Door and the Way, they came back from the spiritual realm with increased wisdom, increased insight, and supernatural power. They exceeded all of the occult shows of power. They traveled beyond what any witch in all of history has said they traveled. They walked thru walls and on water. They transformed the solar system; making the sun stand still, the rain stop for 3 1/2 years, and making darkness cover an area for days. Elijah received fire, boldness, authority to slay occultists of his time, supernatural transportation (the ability to travel 200+ miles without walking, driving a car, or flying in an airplane), and provisional miracles. Moses received bread, quail, guidance, glory, supernatural provision (which made all of the Israelites wealthy), the dividing of the red sea/supernatural protection, the supernatural defeat of his enemies, and so much more. Moses, Elijah, and the other prophets that received miraculous feats from Heaven paid a price.

Following the legal path is VITAL because if you continue to exercise the "back door" routes into the spiritual realm, the doors of Heaven become shut to you. You may have access now, but the Bible tells us that life on Earth is but a vapor; meaning that it is very swift and short in comparison to our lives in the spiritual realm. Deuteronomy 11:17 tells us our consequences for unrighteousness, saying, "for then the anger of the Lord will be kindled against you and he will shut up the heavens, so there will be no rain and the land will yield no fruit; then you will perish quickly off the good land the Lord is giving you." The curse of unrighteousness can be seen in many civilizations where occult practices have prevailed beyond the point of mercy; the news broadcasts famines, high death rates, and high rates of poverty and disease in areas where darkness has been praised beyond the point of mercy and grace.

How You Can Legally Open Spiritual Doors

To open spiritual doors legally, and grant access to the Holy Spirit out of the gates of your spirit, you must commit to:

-Meditating on the Words of YHWH

Take a scripture and anchor it in a physical reality. For example, if you want to open a door in the spirit, you can take a scripture that speaks about opening a door, and physically open a door. As you are opening the physical door, you can quote the scripture, and repeat these actions to anchor the physical and spiritual realities.

-Waiting on YHWH

Focusing your thought on YHWH, and desperately waiting for an intimate encounter with the presence of YHWH opens doors of your soul to release your spirit, and transrelocate you to the presence of YHWH.

-Prayer

Yeshua said we must ask, seek, and knock for spiritual doors to be open. Prayer is the process of asking.

-Fasting

It has been proven that at birth and before death, the DMT hormone levels are so high you can see the spiritual and physical realms simultaneously, then you cross over into the spirit reality for eternity. When you fast, you are crucifying the flesh; dying to self. It is my belief the DMT hormone levels are changed in the process of fasting similar to the process of death allowing you to focus on the spiritual realm and grasp spiritual realities with increased clarity. Fasting has the ability to open the door to the Holy

Spirit and enables you to exercise your privileges as an heir thru your sacrifice.

-Righteousness

You must maintain your cleanliness in order to commune with YHWH. You have to forsake certain activities and commit to following the paths of YHWH. Abiding by the laws of YHWH opens doors, grants opportunities, and multiplies everything you've invested into Heaven. The Bible has given us every direction for healthy eating, relationships with your children, family, and friends. When you abide in the principles given in the word of YHWH, you do not have to be concerned with the callusing of the pineal gland that separates others from communion with YHWH. In articles all across the internet, decalcification of the pineal gland is discussed. Fluoride's found in toothpaste, water, and other foods containing chemicalized waters have been found in autopsies to compile around the pineal gland; inhibiting the interaction between the physical and spiritual realm. Eating the meat, fruits, vegetables, and grains prescribed in the Bible provide the balance our bodies need to properly operate in spiritual and physical planes.

-Sacrifice

Moses sacrificed prestige. He was the heir of the Pharoah of the world power of his day. He chose to forfeit his prestige to carry out the task YHWH has given him to set the Israelites free. His sacrifice took him from success to poverty as YHWH refined him and made modifications to his character, so he could lead His people to their promised land.

-Persistence

Similar to the gold-refining process, we must be refined by tests, trials, and hardships. Thru testing, we are given perseverance, wisdom, might, and stronger character.

-Praise and Worship

In Praise and Worship, you are intertwining the vibrations of your intimate song with the melodies of your soul and spirit. Praise and Worship are a combination on meditating on the greatness of Yeshua and seeing the aerial view of life from Eternity. When you worship, you open yourself up to the Holy Spirit.

-Maintaining a Pure Heart

You can access heavenly places, commune with YHWH, explore Eden, interact with angels, and ride on fiery chariots today, but you DO NOT want to access these places illegally and forfeit your eternal exploration and paradise.

Some Things That You Can Receive From Heaven

Here are some scriptures to show a few things can be received from Heaven when legal routes of access are used:

- Dew

Deuteronomy 33:28:

"So Israel lives in safety, untroubled is Jacob's abode in a land of grain and wine, where the heavens drop down dew."

- Messages

- Rain

Deuteronomy 28:12:

"The Lord will open for you his rich storehouse, the heavens, to give the rain of your land in its season and to bless all your undertakings. You will lend to many nations, but you will not borrow."

- Angels

- Hail

Joshua 10:11:

"As they fled before Israel, while they were going down the slope of Beth-horon, the Lord threw down huge stones from heaven on them as far as Azekah, and they died; there were more who died because of the hailstones than the Israelites killed with the sword."

- Thunder

1 Samuel 2:10

The Lord! His adversaries shall be shattered; the Most High will thunder in heaven. The Lord will judge the ends of the earth; he will give strength to his king, and exalt the power of his anointed."

- Lightning

Exodus 10:22

So Moses stretched out his hand toward heaven, and there was dense darkness in all the land of Egypt for three days.

- Bread

Exodus 16:4

Then the Lord said to Moses, "I am going to rain bread from heaven for you, and each day the people shall go out and gather enough for that day. In that way I will test them, whether they will follow my instruction or not.

- Dread and fear

Deuteronomy 2:25

This day I will begin to put the dread and fear of you upon the peoples everywhere under heaven; when they hear report of you, they will tremble and be in anguish because of you."

- Sun

- Moon

- Stars (including planets)

- Glory

- Darkness

2 Samuel 22:10

He bowed the heavens, and came down; thick darkness was under his feet.

- Fire

2 Kings 1:10

But Elijah answered the captain of fifty, "If I am a man of YHWH, let fire come down from heaven and consume you and your fifty." Then fire came down from heaven, and consumed him and his fifty.

- Whirlwinds

- Chariots of Fire

- Horses Of Fire

2 Kings 2:11

As they continued walking and talking, a chariot of fire and horses of fire separated the two of them, and Elijah ascended in a whirlwind into heaven.

- Power

- Glory

- Victory

- Majesty

1 Chronicles 29:11

Yours, O Lord, are the greatness, the power, the glory, the victory, and the majesty; for all that is in the heavens and on the earth is yours; yours is the kingdom, O Lord, and you are exalted as head above all.

- Judgement

- Righteousness

- Ordinances

- Laws

- Statutes

- Commandments

Nehemiah 9:13

You came down also upon Mount Sinai, and spoke with them from heaven, and gave them right ordinances and true laws, good statutes and commandments,

- Dominion

- Fear

- Peace

Job 25:2

"Dominion and fear are with YHWH; he makes peace in his high heaven.

- Lightning

Job 37:2-4 (NRSV)

Listen, listen to the thunder of his voice and the rumbling that comes from his mouth. Under the whole heaven he lets it loose, and his lightning to the corners of the earth. After it his voice roars; he thunders with his majestic voice and he does not restrain the lightning when his voice is heard.

- Ice and Hoarfrost

Job 38:29

From whose womb did the ice come forth, and who has given birth to the hoarfrost of heaven?

- Love and Faithfulness

Psalm 57:3

He will send from heaven and save me, he will put to shame those who trample on me. Selah YHWH will send forth his steadfast love and his faithfulness.

Psalm 76:8

From the heavens you uttered judgment; the earth feared and was still Heaven has doors that open and close.

Psalms 78:26-27

- Winds

Jeremiah 10:13

When he utters his voice, there is a tumult of waters in the heavens, and he makes the mist rise from the ends of the earth. He makes lightning for the rain, and he brings out the wind from his storehouses.

Jeremiah 49:36

and I will bring upon Elam the four winds from the four quarters of heaven; and I will scatter them to all these winds, and there shall be no nation to which the exiles from Elam shall not come.

- Destroyers

Jeremiah 51:48

Then the heavens and the earth, and all that is in them, shall shout for joy over Babylon; for the destroyers shall come against them out of the north, says the Lord.

- Visions

Ezekiel 1:1

[The Vision of the Chariot] In the thirtieth year, in the fourth month, on the fifth day of the month, as I was among the exiles by the river Chebar, the heavens were opened, and I saw visions of YHWH.

- Flesh

- Birds

He commanded the skies above, and opened the doors of heaven; He caused the east wind to blow in the heavens, and by his power he led out the south wind; he rained flesh upon them like dust, winged birds like the sand of the seas;

- Time: Nehemiah received added time to live on Earth and the Bible tells us that YHWH is the author of time.

For everything there is a season, and a time for every matter under heaven: a time to be born, and a time to die; a time to plant, and a time to pluck up what is planted; a time to kill, and a time to heal; a time to break down, and a time to build up;

Jeremiah 8:7

Even the stork in the heavens knows its times; and the turtledove, swallow, and crane observe the time of their coming; but my people do not know the ordinance of the Lord.

- Word: The Word from Heaven opens portals in the heavens, on the Earth, in our bodies, and in our circumstances.

For as the rain and the snow come down from heaven, and do not return there until they have watered the earth, making it bring forth and sprout, giving seed to the sower and bread to the eater, so shall my word be that goes out from my mouth; it shall not return to me empty, but it shall accomplish that which I purpose, and succeed in the thing for which I sent it.

- Blessing Of The Deep are granted

Deuteronomy 33:13

And of Joseph he said: Blessed by the Lord be his land, with the choice gifts of heaven above, and of the deep that lies beneath;

- Blessings of The Earth (fruit of the land and of the womb) are granted

Haggai 1:10

Therefore the heavens above you have withheld the dew, and the earth has withheld its produce.

- Everything

John 3:27

John answered, "No one can receive anything except what has been given from heaven.

CHAPTER ELEVEN

SEE THE AERIAL VIEW

"Light was created on the first day of creation. The Sun, moon, stars, and galaxies were created on the fourth day of creation. Why are so many people living from fourth day light, subjecting their lives to fourth day light, rather than living from eternal light and first day light which governs the fourth day light?"

-Paraphrased from Ian Clayton's teaching "The Speed of Light"

The Story of Martin and Marie

Martin and his wife, Marie were college graduates. They both had their doctorate degrees and had amassed a lot of debt. In combination, they calculated their school loans would take them 20 years to pay off at their current pay rates with their current living expenses subtracted. They desperately wanted to do something to be free from their debt.

Martin and Marie decided if they applied to live on the Moon, and they received enough interest from others who are curious about their journey, they could start a blog, write books, and make enough extra money to pay their debt off. They began fashioning their future around the hope they would be chosen by NASA to live on the moon. They began considering ideas like how different the time would be, how different the gravitational pull and cooking would be, how different communicating with others would be, and how different it would be to raise their children.

Martin and Marie were beyond ecstatic about life on the moon. They completely changed their spending; purchasing only things that would benefit their new life on the moon, they developed a new system to track time from their aerial view of the moon, and they sat above their earthly worries because they knew they were soon to be erased.

Your Spirit Should Be Seated In Heavenly Places

Similar to Martin and Marie, many people excitedly applied to live on other planets or on the moon. They anticipate the difference in life on another planet, and believe by relocating, they can escape the burdens they experience in their current location. King Solomon said, "There is nothing new under the sun". With this, we know that anything overshadowed by the sun will repeat the patterns we currently see around us regardless of what planet, state, country, or province. The difference happens when we are seated in Heavenly places, and maintaining an aerial view from Eternity. When you are seated in Heavenly places, you will be able to convene with the Father, Son, and Holy Spirit, seven spirits before the throne, and all of the angels that eagerly await the appointed time to provide you with insight. As a result of the insight you receive, you act with authority over your circumstances. Time, creation, obstacles are under your feet when you are seated as you should be. For this reason, scriptures say:

- For creation, serving you who made it, exerts itself to punish the unrighteous, and in kindness relaxes on behalf of those who trust in you (Wisdom 16:24).

- For the creation waits with eager longing for the revealing of the children of YHWH; for the creation was subjected to futility, not of its own will but by the will of the one who subjected it, in hope the creation itself will be set free from its bondage to decay and will obtain the freedom of the glory of the children of YHWH. We know the whole creation has been groaning in labor pains until now; and not only the creation, but we ourselves, who have the first fruits of the Spirit, groan inwardly while we wait for adoption, the redemption of our bodies. (Romans 8: 19-23)

Similar to riding in an airplane, and looking down from above, when you are seated in Heavenly places with the Messiah, the things you view from Earth as mountains become very small. The circumstances that seem overbearing from Earth, you can see around when you are seated where you are supposed to be.

Baptism Into The Nature of YHWH

I have studied varying forms of baptism, and found there are many things YHWH can immerse you into for increased understanding of His infinite nature. There is the baptism into the body of the Messiah, the baptism into the Holy Spirit, the baptism into the Holy Spirit with fire, the baptism in Unity, the baptism in love, and the baptism into the glory cloud (as Moses experienced) amongst others. The Bible tells us YHWH would immerse or fill a person with a facet of His nature for varying reasons.

The book of Exodus shows two profound examples of baptism: the baptism into the glory cloud and the baptism in divine spirit. Exodus 34:5 says:

The Lord descended in the cloud and stood with him there, and proclaimed the name, "The Lord."

Then later in Exodus 34, when a cloud of smoke wrapped Mount Sinai, the people were filled with the fear of the Lord and reverence. Later in Exodus, when YHWH instructed Moses to build the temple of meeting, He filled Bezalel with a divine spirit so he would have the skills necessary to create the utensils, curtains, and other delicacies for the temple. In Exodus alone, you can see people immersed in various facets of the nature of YHWH: reverence, glory, and His divine Spirit. In Acts, the Holy Spirit filled the Disciples of Yeshua so they could proclaim their witness with boldness, and have a unique identity.

The nature of YHWH is infinite and it is necessary to understand the nature of your Father to understand yourself and your role. When you understand the omniscience of YHWH, you can rest in the truth that your spiritual reality prevails over physical phenomena. You should ask YHWH for baptism into His nature in greater and greater doses. Request to be immersed in His truth, His glory, His heart, His love, or other facets of His being. When you are immersed in Him, your aura changes. People can identify you are a foreigner because your ways become peculiar. For this reason, Peter said:

"But you are a chosen race, a royal priesthood, a holy nation, YHWH's own people, in order that you may proclaim the mighty acts of him who called you out of darkness into his marvelous light." (1 Peter 2:9)

Every Culture Has Distinguishing Characteristics

Every country has an identity that is physically apparent among their populace. Some people will be identified as foreigners by their dialect. Others, will be identified by how unfamiliar or uncomfortable they are with common area cuisine. Some people will be very noticeable because of the way they dress. Similar to how cultures can be distinguished amongst others simply by geographic locations, citizens of the Kingdom of Heaven have an identified aura because they are foreign to the Earth.

For Kingdom citizens, there is no fear in their walk and talk; their military is so sure of itself they can invade plunder the fiercest enemies; the ones that initiate the physical traumas. They are humble yet bold, striking and powerful. They wear the auras of a lion, an ox, an eagle, and a man: gentle, understanding, fierce, bold, peculiar, creative, and victorious. They can carry away its Principalities; their powers, and rulers of darkness. They are strangers in foreign soils, they look and act that way, they talk that way, the economic situations of those nations where they are strangers don't bother and affect them, they walk and talk like people from other planets. A Kingdom citizen is a rare commodity and a light to this world.

The Scripture declares you are a stranger and foreigner in this world. When talking about the hope Abraham, Isaac, and Jacob had that they would live in another kingdom completely different than the Earth, Hebrews 11:13-16 says:

All of these died in faith without having received the promises, but from a distance they saw and greeted them. They confessed they were strangers and foreigners on the earth, for people who speak in this way make it clear they are seeking a homeland. If they had been thinking of the land they had left behind, they would have had opportunity to return. But as it is, they desire a better country, that is, a heavenly one. Therefore YHWH is not ashamed to be called their God; indeed, he has prepared a city for them.

You are a person just passing, but who must leave indelible footprints on the path that you tread. You do not belong here, but you are called to influence your path in the order of Melchizedek under the subjection to the High Priest, Yeshua the Messiah.

Yeshua in His own words declared you are not of the world even as He is not of the world; but you also know YHWH so loved the world that He sent Yeshua to die for it; such that though He is and was not of the world yet He never left it without doing something to influence it (See John 17:14 and 3:16). That is your call; that is your purpose for being here.

You should not talk as citizens of everywhere else

One key thing about a people and a nation or state in particular is the language they speak; they are given away by their own tongue, a geographical entities most likely have a common language.

In the kingdom of YHWH, we have a language, we don't talk like everyone else talks. The religious leaders of Yeshua' time sent temple police to arrest Yeshua, when they got there, the Scriptures say they could not lay hands on Yeshua not because of the power that exudes from Him, nor because of angels that surrounded Him but because of the words that were coming out of His mouth-Yeshua learned and spoke kingdom vocabularies. "No man ever spoke like this man, they replied." (See John 7:46) You are to copy Him.

No doubt, fear, or problem-focus should come out of your mouth

The apostles of the Messiah took after Him, they emulated Him so much people who were observing them nicknamed them because they were people like the Messiah, in word and in conduct. They talked like Yeshua would talk, love like Yeshua would love, behaved like Yeshua would; like people from another planet.

They never talked fear; nor doubt, they never talked their weakness and their worries, but always talked victory, strength and ability. You hear them in the midst of trouble saying: Greater is He that is in us than he that is in the world. You hear them in the face of opposition saying: "Yea in all these things we are more than a conqueror through Him that loved us." You hear them shout amidst pressure: For though we are hard pressed on every side, yet not crushed; we are perplexed, but not in despair; persecuted, but not forsaken; struck down, but not destroyed (See 1 John 4:4, Romans 8:37 and 2 Corinthians 4:8-9). They have learned heaven's vocabulary and they are speaking it. Follow their examples!

You should not look like citizens of everywhere else

Yeshua was a perfect and complete representation of the kingdom of YHWH; He was YHWH's ambassador per excellence. The apostles had no other choice than to follow in His example; look like Him, talk like Him, and act like Him.

Their dressing was even typical of Yeshua that they were taking after so much so that Judas with a kiss would have to give away Yeshua to His crucifiers otherwise they would have mistaken Peter, or James and any other of the apostles for Him. They were one in everything.

In our kingdom, there are dress codes, appearance codes, you just don't look like every other person or talk like them. Everything about you gives you away. You carry the mark of fellowship with the Messiah. People can see that you have learned kingdom practices. As we discussed previously when discussing your gates, you live from the Spirit inside of you rather than the body outside of you. You are motivated by the Spirit, rather than the body. Your ideas regarding dress, posture, confidence, esteem, and all else comes from the spirit. You dress as an act of worship; exemplifying the Kingdom you represent. Your will and choices are in submission to the Messiah. You abandon current trends and allow YHWH to mark you with the dignity of the Kingdom in your attire. Confidently answer these questions:

- When you dress, who do you represent?

- Will the Messiah be proud of the way you look if you run into each other on the way?

It matters how you look in the kingdom. For this reason, from the fall of man, YHWH designated the attire. In Exodus, YHWH gave specific regulations regarding attire for priests to enter His presence. The way you conduct yourself, whether in dignity or in cultural trends, reflects who and what you are submitted to.

You should be distinguished and look like you are employed by the greatest King of all

Have you ever seen how servants who wait on kings dress? The queen of Sheba had a glimpse of this on her visit to King Solomon and the Scripture says no breath was left in her when she saw the conduct of Solomon and of his attendants (See 1 Kings 10:1-9).

We are even more distinguished than King Solomon and his palace attendants, we are ambassadors for the Messiah; we are direct representatives of the King of kings and the Lord of lords. We are joint heirs with the Messiah, sharers of his glory and of His grace. We are at the service of the King, and we do it with all the seriousness that we've got.

You should not be shaken as everywhere else because your Kingdom cares for you

We have received a kingdom which cannot be shaken. Hebrews 12:28-19 says, Therefore, since we are receiving a kingdom that cannot be shaken, let us give thanks, by which we offer to YHWH an acceptable worship with reverence and awe; for indeed our YHWH is a consuming fire." When the people of the world are shaken with news of economic collapse, we are not because we know we are strangers and foreigners in this world, our nation's government determines our economy even in the midst of those nations.

When they say there is a casting down, we keep shouting that there is a lifting up, with our face looking up from whence come our help. (Job 22:29 and Psalm 121:2)

Your Finances Should Be Different Than Everyone Else

Donny is a multimillionaire. He did not inherit wealth, but rather, he was raised in a low income neighborhood. His mom was more than the average churchgoer, she believed Yeshua was real, and she boasted of how good he was to her all of the time. She had little expectation for herself, but she had a lot of expectation for Donny. She would always say, "You are going to be the richest man you have ever seen." She would affirm his skills taught him to separate for YHWH a portion of his time and his wealth. Despite the economic climate of his youth, Donny received a lot of affirmation from those around him. He was highly skilled in creating one-of-a-kind events, and his church gave him several high profile opportunities to plan events. By the time that he was 15 years old, he began making over $100,000 per year for event planning, and by the time he was 20, he was a millionaire.

Once he reached multimillionaire status, he began to feel that when he gives tithes or offering to the local church he was the primary reason that it was staying open. He had reinterpreted Malachi 3 to say, "10% of all that comes into your hands is only necessary if your tithe does not cover all of the local church expenses". He felt that since his offering was more than the church building expenses that he could keep the rest for himself. At times when he calculated his tithe, it was in excess of $50,000.00 for one month, and his church building expenses only reached $20,000 monthly. Without a doubt, he knew YHWH used the messages and events of the local church to speak to him, so he could achieve all that he has, but rather than giving his whole tithe to the church, he chose to give $25,000-$30,000 which still covered their building expenses.

Donny started to see vandalism in his dreams, but he had not really believed in dreams, so he didn't pay it any attention. He began having a problem with squirrels making holes and entering into his home. He experienced more food spoilage than ever. He would go to the grocery store and within 5 days the food was all spoiled, so he began spending more on his groceries. His multi-million-dollar mortgage interest rate and property tax increased. Miscellaneous fees kept coming up: he was pulled over by the police, his homeowner's association increased their dues, and he received a lawsuit that could potentially put him out of business. When Donny cried out to YHWH about what was happening in his life, he heard the voice of YHWH say, "I warned you in a dream about vandalism to come. You have robbed me, therefore, I have lifted my hedge of protection from you. I made you the head, but I can easily flip the coin and make you the tail as I have done for those that dishonor me. Choose today what you will do."

Donny repented to YHWH for reinterpreting His word. He began bringing his whole tithe, he gave offerings, and he set aside money for the poor, the widows, and the orphans. His lawsuit was overturned, and his business became increasingly successful. His local church was able to plant more locations and serve more people. He was given increased revelation about how to preserve food and his spoilage was cut down to less than 1% of everything he brought into his house. His property was re-assessed, and the raised taxes were a mistake. He received an offer to refinance, and his interest rate went down. He made a friend who advised him about how to get rid of the squirrel invasion in his house, and peace was restored to him.

Similar to what Donny experienced, all who do not separate what is holy unto YHWH are placed under a curse. The curse that results from disobedience to YHWH is demonstrated by stagnancy despite effort. Maybe you are a multimillionaire like Donny, but even when you increase your effort, your results still remain the same. This is what a curse looks like. Israel demonstrated the curse on their finances in several locations throughout the Bible. In Egypt, when they were slaves, they would work very hard; under harsh conditions, but they were not creating wealth. The same is true in Babylon, they worked, made money, but their income was subject to Babylonian rules.

Curses, Birth Defects, and Demonic Activity Should Be Lifted From Your Financial Affairs

While the world is experiencing volatility as money is their god, as an ambassador of the Kingdom of Heaven, you should be having a different experience. The YHWH you serve is the creator and maker of all. He makes all connections, all revelation, all solutions, and all prosperity. When the world around you is tossing like the waves of the sea, you should be demonstrating the evidence your King is the Provider of all Providers.

Poverty and debt are curses

Deuteronomy 28:47-49 says, "Because you did not serve the Lord your YHWH joyfully and gladly in the time of prosperity, therefore in hunger and thirst, in nakedness and dire poverty, you will serve the enemies the Lord sends against you. He will put an iron yoke on your neck until he has destroyed you. The Lord will bring a nation against you from far away, from the ends of the earth, like an eagle swooping down, a nation whose language you will not understand" In other words, poverty and slavery are curses that result from dishonoring YHWH with your wealth. Poor stewardship leads to spiritual debt and dissatisfaction. Honor YHWH with your wealth and experience true prosperity.

Identify The Spiritual Root if You Have Financial Dysfunction or Dissatisfaction

Many people realize the supernatural influence behind miracles, but they are inattentive to the supernatural influence behind curses. Curses place you at a standstill; low or no increase. Most people attribute this stagnancy to a superficial reason, rather than looking deeper at the spiritual origin to the physical manifestation. Everything begins in the Spirit first, and a curse is like a wall where a blessing is a bridge or an open door. Which do you want?

In his teaching called, "Identifying the Strongman", Apostle Renny Mclean said that most people (even Christian people) have a difficult time identifying the spiritual defects they were born with. He said most people know where they are born, but they have never inquired about the spiritual condition they were born with. In response, I want to ask you, "Are you in the same economic state as the generations before you? Are you implementing the same practices that those that preceded you have? Were you born with a spiritual financial precursor?" Most people pray for YHWH to cancel superficial issues like debt or dissatisfaction with material rather than going deeper and rebuking the spirit of lust or envy beneath the surface. Identify the strongman, repent for giving him access (even if it is a generational curse), and pray to YHWH; removing his access from your future. Matthew 12:45 says, "Then it goes and takes with it seven other spirits more wicked than itself, and they go in and live there. The final condition of that person is worse than the first. That is how it will be with this wicked generation." When dissected, one will find that the word, "house" can mean 3 things depending on which language you translate to. Being that the Bible was written in Hebrew and Greek, Apostle Mclean dissected the scripture with these two translations. In Greek, "house" means "Generation". In Hebrew "house" can mean "tent" or "temporal residence". With the translation in mind, we know when the demon said, "I will go back to my house", it does not only mean your flesh, but also the generational vision to which he came. For example, many African American people suffer curses from slavery. Violence, incest, and other evils are deeply rooted in family lineages. Churches are casting out symptoms or the seven demons that came to protect the vision of the original, and are not identifying and casting out the strong man. Seek YHWH, identify the strong man, and remove his access from your life!

It's important to identify the triggering spiritual factor for your financial crises. Beyond revelation (which I am sure you increased by reading this book), is a relationship with YHWH, and the receipt of his gift of discerning spirits. Apostle Mclean said that most people are not able to identify when a physical symptom has come from demonic torment versus a curse versus a birth defect, but let me briefly explain.

The fruits of the flesh are simply superficial evidences of demonic attack; they cannot be cast out because they are only the fruits. All of the fruits lead to fulfillment, poverty (in the long term), and spiritual death. Galatians 5:19-21 tells us that they are, "sexual immorality, impurity and debauchery; idolatry and witchcraft; hatred, discord, jealousy, fits of rage, selfish ambition, dissensions, factions and envy; drunkenness, orgies, and the like. I warn you, as I did before, that those who live like this will not inherit the kingdom of YHWH." Even deeper than the fruit is the tree (the demon that planted the seed of rebellion and deceit). Sometimes, the demonic entry can come from family ties, association (generational, workplace, or friendship), or from personal decision-making. When you have identified the fruit, you know demonic activity is taking place; either possession (taking control of the body) or oppression (influencing the body without taking it captive).

A curse is a supernatural mandate of YHWH created as a consequence for those who do not abide by the laws of the Kingdom of Heaven. Deuteronomy 28:15 says, "However, if you do not obey the Lord your Elohim (only God) and do not carefully follow all his commands and decrees I am giving you today, all these curses will come on you and overtake you". Accordingly, the Bible tells of curses that are evident in the finances because people have not honored YHWH with their wealth.

A birth defect is something that resulted from an attack in the womb. Job 15:34-35 says, "For the company of the godless will be barren, and fire will consume the tents of those who love bribes. They conceive trouble and give birth to evil; their womb fashions deceit." With his, we know that the womb is made accessible to demonic activity by poor choices of the parents. Spiritual and physical birth defects come from an attack in the womb.

It's possible you may see evidences of a curse, a birth defect, or demonic activity in your life, and I have good news! When Yeshua died on the cross, and descended into Sheol, he carried the sins and curses of the world. When he demonstrated he had conquered all potential opposition of man to include poverty and death, he enabled you to trample the same opposition underfoot. You have been given the authority to trample poverty, release yourself from demonic strongholds, and to resurrect dead areas of your life (your creativity, your intellect, your physical ability, or even your willpower). If you have identified a curse, a birth defect, or demonic activity, I want to lead you in prayer right now. Let's activate the resurrection power in you right now! Say this prayer aloud:

Father, I have come to a deeper realization of your majesty, your power, your glory, and your design for my life. I confess that I have fallen short of your assignment for me on this Earth, and I now understand what Yeshua did for me when He died on the cross and rose again. I believe that Yeshua rose, and I thank you for the resurrection power that you have given me. I declare that from today on, I will exercise my authority as your ambassador on this Earth. I invite your Kingdom to come in every area of my life, and I submit myself as your vessel to advance your Kingdom thru the Earth. I vow to crucify my flesh daily and instead to walk in Yours. Provide for me this day everything that I need to succeed in my assignment. I loose from captivity everyone who I hold hostage in unforgiveness, and I request that you cleanse me from all evil: cancel demonic activity, cancel curses, and resurrect any dead areas of my life. Lead me closer to you, and guide me away from evil in Yeshua' name. Amen.

Give YHWH the First fruits Of All That Comes Into Your Hands

My husband and I have personally found the most paramount prosperity law of all is to separate what is holy; this we have learned thru hardship. On occasion, we have withheld our tithes because doubt arose because we lean on our own understanding. In every instance, disaster struck in mysterious ways until we confessed our wrong to YHWH, and aligned our will and our actions to the Word of YHWH. Today, I want to recommend this to you! Give Him the first fruits of your heart and your finances, and see how He pours blessing on you!

Do not be dependent on the ways or functions of the world

I have never seen an ambassador that depends on the nation where he serves for His supplies and sustenance; I have never met one who allows the influences of the nation of its residence to determine his or her actions. On the contrary, the ambassador tries to exert his nation's and kingdom's influence on the people where he serves.

I believe this was what Paul had in mind when he wrote in Romans 12:2: "Do not be conformed to this world." Do not adopt the practices of the world, do not do things the way the world does, for though we are in the world, we do not belong in the world and we should not function like they do.

The world's way and pattern is different from ours, theirs is subject to change and to failure, but ours is unbreakable, enduring and eternal. Their laws and principles are ephemeral, but ours are eternally enduring. We would cheapen ourselves to copy, pattern and to depend on the way the world does its things.

The world's way is subject to failure, it must fail, and nothing will stop it. Nations are fighting for sustainable growth and commerce now because money has failed. In the world whatever goes up must come down, but in the kingdom, we have infinite possibilities for increase with no gravitational pull to come down.

Do not idolize material

It is important that in the Kingdom, we get a true perspective of materialism. It is the man that is poor that goes to a party and eats with his two hands; and even takes some home to have to eat for another day. But the person who always has enough to eat all the time, will only eat a mouth full; that will be all for him. He is not afraid whether he will have to eat tomorrow or not.

In the kingdom of YHWH, an understanding of who we are and what we have is important, our source never runs dry, our Father owns the cattle upon a thousand hills; the gold and the silver are His and are ours for the enjoyment.

We know we are rich and loaded, we were born into the wealthiest family in the universe and so we don't go stealing or majoring on the family wealth, it is ours nonetheless. We just take and enjoy it. We are blessed with all spiritual blessings in the heavenly places in Yeshua, the Bible says. Ephesians 1:3 says, "Blessed be the Elohim and Father of our Lord Yeshua the Messiah, who has blessed us in Him with every spiritual blessing in the heavenly places".

The things that you physically see will always fail you

The great Apostle to the gentile-Paul knew about this secret of the kingdom we are talking about today, putting it in His own words he said: while we do not look at the things which are seen, but at the things which are not seen. For the things which are seen are temporary, but the things which are not seen are eternal. (2 Corinthians 4:18). Things that are temporal fade with time and with use but things that are unseen are eternal and endure beyond time.

Only YHWH cannot disappoint

I have seen the rich in this world go broke and poor and I have also seen the poor getting rich. Nations have risen and fallen, kingdoms have come and gone, economies have been superpower and are no more today but the kingdom of YHWH abides forever.

YHWH's unchanging nature guarantees the stability of His kingdom, so with gratitude, we need to walk in the confidence as the ambassador of the greatest King of all; for there is no failure with YHWH.

CHAPTER TWELVE

MAKE TREATIES

I see all through the Scriptures, the people of the covenant making pacts and treaties with the inhabitants of the places where they go or live and I know this is a very important aspect of the kingdom of YHWH. From Abraham to Isaac and even onto the Judges and the occupation of the land of promise, pacts are parts and parcel of their national existence, polity and survival.

What is a pact or treaty? According to Webster's 1828 dictionary, a treaty is an agreement, league or contract between two or more nations or sovereigns, formally signed by commissioners properly authorized, and solemnly ratified by the several sovereigns or the supreme power of each state. In a nutshell, a treaty in whatever form holds on the ground of legality-it must be backed by law, signed and sealed as agreed upon by the sovereign nations.

We as YHWH's ambassadors and commissioners are saddled with the responsibility to make holy treaties for the kingdom among the nations we go serve.

Tell the Kings how to transform their Kingdoms

You are a teacher and instructor of nations and kingdoms as a true representative of your nation. The nations are to learn from you how to rule in righteousness and make judgment with equity.

The United States always suggests programs and agendas to any free nations on earth where they are present that are met for the transformation of those nations. Many nations want to learn from the US how they have become what they are. How much more would every kingdom need to learn successful strategy from a kingdom that has never failed? Nations learn from you and I, ambassadors of YHWH's glorious kingdom, how YHWH rules over 7 billion inhabitants of the earth plus billions of angels and galaxies without having to mess up everything and without having to go on recess not even for a day.

Yeshua gave the world a transformation agenda in the Sermon on the Mount, called the beatitudes. If individual and nations imbibe that agenda, the world would be a better place. Let us teach the nations that agenda.

Submit their cares to YHWH

He will supply for their Kingdom. Yeshua gave a three chapter exhaustive transformation agenda to the world as recorded in Matthew chapters 5, 6 and 7; one of such program covers the area of prayers that guarantees supplies. We are to teach the nations how to bring their fears and worries to the Lord and He will supply and fix their fears. No one governs with YHWH and losses, not even a nation. His supplies are limitless.

Place your King on the throne

The success and strength of a people is the glory of the King. If a kingdom falls to another, it sure means her king has fallen, shame and reproach has covered him, he is a servant now to the power that has overrun him. But when a kingdom is standing tall and strong, it the glory of her king; the wealth of the citizens is influenced by the wealth of their king and the wealth of the king is a sure sign that her subjects are making headways. King Solomon made silver and gold common during his reign as King in Israel. If a man does that, how about YHWH the King over the entire universe?

When we exalt Him, he lifts us up. (See Matthew 6:33)

Place YHWH as supreme in their Kingdom and the benefits will be theirs

There is no nation where YHWH rules and one will not see the fruits of righteousness and justice. His grace and glory and wealth will be lavished upon that nation. Israel is a proof of this in Old Testament times; and YHWH has not changed. (See Psalm 33:12) A nation that extol king Yeshua will reap the benefits of righteousness, for he will rule and reign in peace and righteousness over that land, with fruits of abundance to show for it. Let's tell them so.

Share the testimonies of the Kings that have accepted Heaven's policies and succeeded in their Kingdoms before. The Bible shares story after story of Kings that accepted and adopted heavens policies for their national economy and they succeeded.

David employed the order of heaven in running his government and not one time was it recorded that he failed. In short, the kingdom of Israel was properly established in His time. Solomon took after his father and recorded the same success and much more.

King Josiah and Hezekiah were not left behind, at one time or the other they came up with reform programs which embrace YHWH's policies and ideologies and they recorded success at the end of the day. (See 1 Sam17-2 Sam, 1 Kings 1-11, 2 Kings 21-23, 18-20)

There is a very important and if not the most important task of our kingdom, it is what I called divine enlistment through partnership. Our king will be happy and satisfied with us only to the degree to which we exert His influence on the nationals that we go work among and how much of them we are able to make into immigration citizens.

The United States and Canada have immigration programs every year through which many foreign nationals moved to the United State to settle and to live as citizens. They are copying YHWH.

YHWH has granted us permission to issue Green Cards to the nationals amongst whom we live. This is our work and we do it through YHWH's mighty energy that is effectively at work in us. (See Colossians 1:28-29) But to assure of success there are some things we need to know:

Be bold

The greatest secret of the success of our kingdoms' ambassadors is boldness; every ambassador knows this and walks it. The early ambassadors of the Kingdom immediately after Yahshua knew this secret. They were bold and courageous. And even the people could see it. Courage is tangible and can be seen. So get a fresh baptism of the spirit of boldness and get to work

Share your testimony

With courage under your breath, you are ready to share your faith and testimony. The king has determined proselytizing in the kingdom being done by word of mouth-people telling people.

Tell what YHWH has done, share the good news of the finished work of Yahshua and by that way, the seeds of the kingdom are sown and multiplied.

By recognizing who is King, they can be citizens. No paperwork. No expensive payments or plans! And for us in this kingdom, not too much of protocols to be a citizen, all one needs is to acknowledge the King by making an open-verbal-allegiance to commit to the king; once that is done, citizenship is granted.

Show them the laws

We do have codes and laws that operate in our kingdom but they are not hard and fast rules as it were, our government operates a liberal economy with lots and lots of liberty. The Bible houses the laws of the kingdom, and we must show them that.

Show them how to access their benefits. So much is entrenched in our constitution as benefits, rights and privileges of the citizenries of the kingdom with just a common key for all to access them-faith. To him that believes, all things are possible; for without it (faith), it is impossible to please YHWH. (Mark 9:23 and Hebrews 11:6)

Share with them how you have accessed yours

There is no selfishness in our kingdom; we share everything and anything. The roads we have passed through we show those coming behind us how to walk through them. As ambassadors we know a lot and have seen a lot, so we know the way and we show the day. Do not hide anything.

Show them how to get justice

There is an opposition to our kingdom, he understands the working of the kingdom because he was one time a staff and an ambassador of the kingdom but who through pride and arrogance rebelled, and our king chased him away. He will always come to trip and to trouble the citizens of the kingdom, but he is an alien and his attempt and works are all illegal. When he comes to you as a citizen of the kingdom, you can deal with Him through the Sword of the Spirit and the name of Yeshua. So you have got to know what the constitution says. It is through it that every citizen on his or her own gets justice for themselves. The book are on your side, the King is on your side, there is an Attorney-General who is waiting on you-on your side, the family lawyer (Yeshua), victory and triumph is assured always in the court of the kingdom, only that you have got to know what is written in the book.

Introduce them to their allies and how to properly send them on assignment

Angels are on the side of the citizens; they heed and do the Father's bidding for us. They are our friends and fellow workers in the kingdom; they are with us in their numbers and strength. All they need is the word of YHWH declared through our mouths and they will be out there doing the word, working for us.

Introduce them to their opponents and how to conquer them

The opposition we face is real and tangible, the host and hordes of darkness are all out to trip us at every instance and to get us down in condemnation and guilt, but through the blood of Yeshua and the power of name, we can always have them crawling at our feet.

There are demons to face; there are even human oppositions that we would come in close contact with, but with the Sword of the Spirit, we'll win.

Connect them to the gifts of the Kingdom

Our king never leaves us destitute of abilities and gifting, when He calls us to service, He furnishes us with abilities. Some of which are:

Talents: We are gifted and talented in the kingdom. Your talents are your natural gifts and endowments, things that you were born with. Some of us came singing from the womb-blessed with beautiful voices, some of us are blessed with flexible bodies that can do any dance in the world, you came with it; use it for the glory of the King.

Passions: Our passions are our zeal and vehement desires, things that unless we do, we will not go to our grave happy. Some people have passion for justice, YHWH gave it to you. Get a degree in law.

Spiritual gifts: We are blessed in the family so much so that our Father and King, does not only endow us with natural abilities (ones we can control because they are part of our makeup), but He also graces us with spiritual gifts, supernatural (beyond the natural) gifts and abilities. The Scripture has a list of them, with 9 that are top of the list of these gifts but yet there are more than 9 in actuality. (See 1 Cor. 12, and Romans 12)

Introduce them to their family

Isolation kills in the kingdom, believers are to flock together as birds of a feather do. So in the kingdom, we walk and work together. We are family and in a family, some of which are already in heaven, while all others are here on earth.

All over the world this family is represented in numbers of local churches and assemblies. In those places we find our fitting and usefulness in the kingdom. You must belong in one at least.

We belong in a set apart assembly called the body of the Messiah; the man Yeshua is the head of that body while you and I that believe are the parts and members of that body. Some of us are the ears of the body, others are the hands, still others are the feet, you are a member of that body and I am a member of it too.

We work in a system as the natural human body is; the brain must communicate to the hand and feet and other parts of the body what needs done and they without objection must do their part. The eye cannot do what the nose was made to do. So take your place in the universal body of the Messiah while finding expression through your local assembly.

Do not place yourself as an idol between man and YHWH

We are ambassadors for the Messiah and not the Messiah ourselves. We do not take the place of our King wherever He sent us. The moment an ambassador starts to present his own interest and veered from the interest and agenda of the government he represents, then you can be sure the sending government will relieve him of his job.

He has broken ties with his country; he has betrayed his nation and has placed personal interest above national interest. As such, His letter of appointment will be withdrawn and repatriated back to his country in most cases.

He is liable; his government can no longer trust him. So as ambassadors of the kingdom, we must not bring ourselves to this depraved shameful level, our King demands and requires our 100 percent loyalty. The King's interest must be first and foremost and when matters of personal interest come in conflict with the King's and the Kingdom's, the King's take the preeminence.

We must not make ourselves the objects and pride of our kingdom but the king and Him alone. So all attention must go to Him and all glory, praise must be His, we must sing His praise and not ours. The King's wrath can be as strong as his love, so let us as ambassador not place ourselves in the stead of YHWH among the tribes He deployed us to as his representatives.

Satan tried to take attention away from YHWH and he was de-throned

The book has a record of one of the King's ex appointee who decided to draw attention to himself; the King dealt with him mercilessly. He is still dealing with him even today. His example is for us to follow, such that we would know no matter how highly placed we are in the cabinet of the King and in his service, we must not fall for insubordination.

The king does not joke with insubordination; He demands and desires complete loyalty and allegiance. We must be wise and dedicated ambassadors.

Many others have followed his lead (including many in church leadership today)

It is worth reiterating here: the king does not condone insubordination. He did not with angels, and He will not with humans. The devil has plotted the fall of so many church founders and leaders through this spirit of insubordination and as it was measured out to Satan so has YHWH also measured out to them; this is because His word is unchanging-YES and AMEN for time and for eternity.

Stay submitted to YHWH and redirecting attention to Him. The more honor(s) we have of the King and the more placed we are in His cadre, the more and most humble we should be-a word for the wise, a key to longevity of service for the ambassador.

DIVINE COMMISSION FOR BEING A KINGDOM OF HEAVEN AMBASSADOR

If you take the advice from this book, you are sure to find the doors Satan uses to enter into your life. Use the tools in this book to close those doors. When the glory from the inside of you comes out, your flesh is transcended, and the glory becomes your covering. With your flesh in submission to the glory, you can begin to notice, that currency will multiply because it will not be spent on unnecessary uses, your health will transform, your relationships will be renewed, and the workings of your life will wear the mark of Yeshua with Shalom. Implement the message, so you can walk into the covenant promises of YHWH. I trust you have enjoyed reading thru this book and you have gained insight for how you can have success in your deployment to the Earth. Heaven and all of its glory is the righteous Ambassador's inheritance! YHWH created you to implement.

In 1 Maccabees, we learn the story of the Greek Empire oppressing the Israelite people. Antiochus Epiphanes was the Greek ruler of Jerusalem. Solomon had built a large temple and dedicated it to the worship of YHWH, and a remnant of Jews dedicated themselves to worshipping YHWH only. Many pagan customs became common in their area, but the remnant decided regardless of the darkness around them, they would still dedicate themselves to the worship of the YHWH of Heaven.

This book has instructed you on how you can also make the decision to consecrate yourself in spite of the darkness around you. Yeshua foretold the end times to be like the times of Noah. With this, we know that evil will be common, and a small remnant will choose to remove the altars of Baal, Ashtoreth, and all other pagan gods. I am hoping that remnant is you.

After much battle, Judas Maccabees led the Jews to victory. Thru battle, they won their temple back, but that was not the end. Antiochus Epiphanes had defiled the temple by sacrificing unclean animals on their altars, misusing their holy items, and bringing debauchery into the sanctuary; the temple was a bloody, semen-filled, and idol infested place.

If you are going thru this journey for the first time, you may be like me, I was the defiled temple. I could completely relate to the mess that the Jews were left to clean up. I had a defiled imagination, a broken heart, an untamed tongue, an infested diet, and many other things that needed cleaning. 1 Maccabees 1:41-58 tells us that the Israelites:

1. Removed all of the defiled stones regardless of how heavy or how much effort it took to remove them

2. They tore down their defiled altars

3. They built holy altars as instructed by YHWH

4. They rebuilt the sanctuary, the inside of the temple, and the consecrated courts

5. They made new holy vessels and brought them in the

temple

6. They offered incense on the altar

7. Lit their lampstand

8. Placed bread on their table

9. Hung the curtains

1 Maccabees 1:52-58 says:

Early in the morning on the twenty-fifth day of the ninth month, which is the month of Chislev, in the one hundred forty-eighth year, they rose and offered sacrifice, as the law directs, on the new altar of burnt offering that they had built. At the very season and on the very day that the Gentiles had profaned it, it was dedicated with songs and harps and lutes and cymbals. All the people fell on their faces and worshiped and blessed Heaven, who had prospered them. So they celebrated the dedication of the altar for eight days, and joyfully offered burnt offerings; they offered a sacrifice of well-being and a thanksgiving offering. They decorated the front of the temple with golden crowns and small shields; they restored the gates and the chambers for the priests, and fitted them with doors. There was very great joy among the people, and the disgrace brought by the Gentiles was removed.

Similar to their process for rededicating the temple of YHWH. You need to maintain your temple dedicated to YHWH. Perform the above steps (as instructed in the book), and dedicate your temple to YHWH. A scripture to meditate on to dedicate yourself to YHWH:

When the priests came out of the holy place, the cloud filled the Lord's temple, and because of the cloud, the priests were not able to continue ministering, for the glory of the Lord filled the temple.

Then Solomon said:
The Lord said that He would dwell in thick darkness.
I have indeed built an exalted temple for You,
a place for Your dwelling forever.

-1 Kings 8:10-13

Thick darkness is created by the merge of two separate frequencies of light, two different molecule structures; it's the shadow of Heaven. Darkness does not always imply evil, it can also mean the merge of a different realm that the enemy cannot tolerate.

Affirmation:

It is written the temple of Solomon was filled with your glory so much that it overshadowed their ministry. You said that you dwell in thick darkness. I dedicated my temple to you, and invite you to dwell here forever.

May YHWH order your steps, so that you can administer and manifest the Kingdom of Heaven everywhere that you go now!

-**Tiffany Domena**

ABOUT THE AUTHOR

Tiffany Domena is an Ambassador of the Kingdom of Heaven, wife, mother, bestselling author, and advocate for living your life by YHWH's design. Bringing nine years of military experience, an educational background in Bible (Bachelor's in Religion along with some graduate coursework), and a Biblical worldview, Tiffany enjoys training others on how to be successful in their deployments to the Earth. She is the founder at Kingdom of Heaven Ambassadors International where her primary focus is taking enemy territory back on the internet and in mainstream media, and refocusing hearts and minds on Yeshua the Messiah. Expertly publishing ten books, hosting a podcast, and blogging on pertinent topics that strike our world, Tiffany's passion bleeds thru her work, and encourages those who get wind of her. She has been known to speak and write on topics including prayer, life purpose, marriage, sex, temptation, goal-setting, wisdom, and prosperity. Other books by Tiffany include:

- 12 Undeniable Laws For Prosperity

- 12 Undeniable Laws For Marriage

- 12 Undeniable Laws For Being Wise As A Snake

- 12 Undeniable Laws For Prayer

- 12 Undeniable Laws For Sex

- Perception: The World's Most Affluent Leader and companion workbook

- Transform Your Habits To Create Your Position of Power Workbook

- Someone Covets You

Find more resources, training, or to subscribe to Tiffany's blog, podcast, or social network, visit www.kingdomofheavenambassador.com.

ONE LAST THING...

If you enjoyed this book, I would love to hear! I personally read all reviews written on my books, and I use them to make the books better and more effective. I would greatly appreciate your feedback at the links below:

Amazon Link:

http://www.amazon.com/Tiffany-Domena/e/B00MSHE0LI

Website Link:

http://www.kingdomofheavenambassador.com/shop/

Goodreads Link:

https://www.goodreads.com/author/show/8459952.Tiffany_Domena

May YHWH bless you!

Tiffany Domena

www.ingramcontent.com/pod-product-compliance
Lightning Source LLC
LaVergne TN
LVHW051115080426
835510LV00018B/2044